Brett General Contracting, LLC

v.

The School Board of Nita County

Case File

Trial Materials

Brett General Contracting, LLC

v.

The School Board of Nita County

Case File

Trial Materials

Marni Becker-Avin
Professional Development and Marketing Program Administrator
Becker & Poliakoff

Beth Thomas
Director of Litigation Technology and Support (Retired)

NITA®
National Institute for Trial Advocacy

Address inquiries to:
Reprint Permission
National Institute for Trial Advocacy
357 McCaslin Blvd., Suite 200
Louisville, CO 80027
Phone: (800) 225-6482
Email: publications@nita.org

ISBN 979-8-88669-182-5
FBA 2182
eISBN 979-8-88669-183-2
eFBA 2183

ASPEN PUBLISHING

Official co-publisher of NITA.
aspenpublishing.com/NITA

Contents

Acknowledgments

The authors would like to acknowledge and thank their NITA faculty, including MJ Barr, Stuart Reynolds, and John Farrell, who have been teaching at BPU since its inception, and Monique Carter, who joined us later but has contributed no less. Their guidance and expertise have been invaluable throughout the years.

This case file was originally prepared for Becker & Poliakoff, P.A. for their annual advocacy program, which is in its 19th year as of 2026. The authors thank Becker for the opportunity to write this case study and for providing it to other attorneys to use for their litigation programs. To learn more about Becker, visit www.beckerlawyers.com.

Case Summary

Plaintiff Brett General Contracting, LLC (Brett), located in Nita County, is suing Defendant, the School Board of Nita County (SBNC), for breach of contract and bad faith after SBNC refused to pay delay-related change order costs. Defendant is countersuing for breach of contract.

Because this is a civil case, Brett has the burden of proving each of the causes of action by a preponderance of the evidence. The last cause of action, bad faith, requires a higher standard than negligence, and must be willful/intentional.

With regard to the affirmative defenses, SBNC has a burden of persuasion. SBNC must raise sufficient facts such that Brett must address the affirmative defense. The burden of proof, however, remains with Brett. In regard to the counterclaim, SBNC has the burden of proof and must prove its counterclaim beyond a preponderance of the evidence.

Brett's complaint alleges that SBNC hired it to do a project, that Plaintiff completed the project, and that SBNC will not pay the final change order for delay damages.

Brett alleges that it has done dozens of projects over the past twenty years for SBNC with no problems. It is familiar with SBNC's procedures and the form contract. Brett admits that it knows and acknowledges that there is a "no damage for delay" clause and an active interference clause, which says that it does not matter who caused the delay. The contract states that contractors get no money for delays; however, it does list some exceptions. Brett admits that it was paid for all change order costs, with the exception of the delay costs for being on the jobsite longer than anticipated by the contract.

Brett alleges that the first project manager, Thomas Smith, who was an SBNC employee, disappeared for weeks at a time because of illness, caused the delay, and promised to pay for the delay damages. Brett also alleges that second project manager, Carol Marks, also a school board employee, agreed to the delay costs in writing.

Brett alleges it fronted the money for multiple costs and relied on SBNC's promises that these costs would be paid. Brett claims SBNC is now hiding behind a technicality. Brett is claiming bad faith based on project manager Marks writing a note about paying the change orders.

Brett claims SBNC approved the handwritten note. SBNC argues that they never even saw the note so they could not have approved it.

SBNC answers that they have sovereign immunity and no employee can bind them to anything that was not voted on by the school board. SBNC also now counterclaims for breach of contract.

SBNC's project manager, Marks, emailed Brett on two occasions requesting ETA of construction project completion date, due to the fast approaching school year opening.

Brett completed the project and advised SBNC of the completion and again requested final payment of the LLC's out-of-pocket delay costs.

CASE SUMMARY

Instructions for Use as a Full Trial

When this case file is used as the basis for a full trial, the parties may call the following witnesses:

Plaintiff Brett General Contracting, LLC:

- Richard Brett
- First project manager Thomas Smith

Defendant School Board of Nita County:

- Superintendent of Schools Robert Franklin, Jr.
- Second project manager Carol Marks
- SBNC board member Holly Williams

Optional expert witnesses:

- Involved expert witness: architect Sonia Forester, We Build Nita, Inc.
- General contractor Eric Mayper

All years in these materials are stated in the following form:

YR-0 indicates the actual year in which the case is being tried (i.e., the present year).

YR-1 indicates the next preceding year (please use the actual year).

YR-2 indicates the second preceding year (please use the actual year), etc.

Color electronic exhibits can be found at the following website:

bit.ly/43axcZr
Password: Brett1

Stipulations

All depositions were properly reviewed and signed by the deponents.

The construction contract mentioned in the complaint and answer as Exhibit A was appropriately attached to these pleadings. It appears in this case file's exhibit section as Exhibit 1.

In YR-3, Nita State suffered a bird flu pandemic that resulted in a strict quarantine for six weeks and social distancing restrictions for nine months. Thanks to the valiant efforts of the Nita State citizens, this pandemic was contained in the state and neighboring states did not experience illness. During Nita's bird flu pandemic, there were no Paycheck Protection Program (PPP) loans or other government offsets to assist companies with payroll.

Pleadings

IN THE STATE OF NITA
NITA COUNTY CIRCUIT COURT

BRETT GENERAL CONTRACTING, LLC, a Nita corporation, Plaintiff, v. THE SCHOOL BOARD OF NITA COUNTY, Defendant.	CASE NO. 2-31869(12)(B)

COMPLAINT

Plaintiff, BRETT GENERAL CONTRACTING, LLC, a Nita corporation ("BRETT"), brings this action against the Defendant, THE SCHOOL BOARD OF NITA COUNTY ("SBNC"), and states that they are entitled to relief based upon the following facts:

GENERAL ALLEGATIONS

1. This is an action for damages in excess of $15,000.00, exclusive of interest, costs, and attorneys' fees and is otherwise within the jurisdiction of this court.

2. BRETT is a Nita corporation authorized to do business in Nita as a contractor, with its principal place of business in Nita County, Nita.

3. SBNC is a political subdivision of the State of Nita in Nita County.

4. Venue is proper in Nita County since SBNC is located in Nita County, Nita, and the causes of action asserted accrued in said county.

5. On or about March 10, YR-3, BRETT entered into a contract with SBNC to perform construction services including furnishing labor and materials for the improvement of the real property ("the project") known as Alan B. Whitfield Elementary School, located at 1532 Nita Road, Nita City, Nita 57818. A true and correct copy of this contract is attached as Exhibit A.

6. The project consisted of remodeling and construction of a cafeteria and eight classroom additions to Alan B. Whitfield Elementary School. The contract price for the project was $5,218,000.00.

7. During the course of construction at Alan B. Whitfield Elementary School, BRETT incurred numerous issues, including problems with the building design and failure of SBNC to timely authorize change orders for required changes on the project, including changes in scope and extensions of time. In addition, BRETT encountered unforeseen

conditions on the project. All of these matters substantially delayed BRETT in performing the project.

8. SBNC, through the actions of its facilities department, interfered with the project's progress in breach of its implied duty not to prevent, hinder, or impede the contractor in the performance of its work. The interference was active, intentional, and went beyond inattention, lethargy, or bureaucracy.

9. As the direct and proximate result of the interference by SBNC, BRETT had to perform additional work on the project. In addition, completion dates for the construction of the project were severely impacted.

10. The interference by SBNC could not have been reasonably anticipated by BRETT.

11. BRETT was entitled to

    a. time extensions for the completion of the project,

    b. recovery of the extra costs and general condition, and

    c. damages for delay caused by SBNC's poor contract administration, interference, and delays.

12. SBNC staff acknowledged that BRETT incurred additional costs and delays resulting from SBNC's interference and poor contract administration. SBNC promised to compensate BRETT for the delays, interference, and additional work. SBNC granted BRETT extensions of time for the completion of the project, but SBNC refused to honor its promise and obligation to compensate BRETT for the additional work and delays on the project.

13. SBNC materially breached the contract by, without limitation:

    a. Failing to timely respond to requests for information;

    b. Failing to compensate BRETT for services rendered and costs incurred resulting from delays SBNC caused;

    c. Actively interfering with the performance of the contractor's work; and

    d. Breaching its implied obligation not to hinder or impede the contractor's performance.

COUNT I—BREACH OF CONTRACT

14. BRETT realleges the allegations of paragraphs 1–13.

15. As a result of the breach of contract, BRETT has suffered damages in excess of $15,000.00.

16. BRETT has been forced to retain the services of the undersigned attorneys to represent it in this action and has agreed to pay attorneys' fees and costs for this representation. BRETT is entitled to an award of its attorneys' fees and costs pursuant to the contract.

WHEREFORE, BRETT demands judgment against Defendant for damages, interest, attorneys' fees, costs of this action and such further relief as this court deems appropriate.

COUNT II—BAD FAITH

17. BRETT realleges the allegations of paragraphs 1–16.

18. As a result of SBNC's bad faith, BRETT has suffered damages.

19. BRETT was forced to retain the services of the undersigned attorneys to represent them in this action and has agreed to pay attorneys' fees and costs for representation. BRETT is entitled to an award of its attorneys' fees and costs pursuant to the contract.

WHEREFORE, SBNC demands judgment against Defendant for damages, interest, attorneys' fees, costs of this action, and such further relief as this court deems appropriate.

DEMAND FOR JURY TRIAL

BRETT hereby demands a trial by jury of all issues so triable in this action.

DATED at Nita County, Nita on October 1st, YR-2.

LAW OFFICES
BOCK, BOCK, & ASSOCIATES
ATTORNEYS FOR PLAINTIFF
1251 Main Street, Suite 2500
Nita City, Nita 57818
(819) 555-1200 – Telephone
(819) 555-7800 – Facsimile

By: /s/ Ernie Bock
Ernie Bock, Jr., Esq.
Nita Bar No. 092893

IN THE STATE OF NITA
NITA COUNTY CIRCUIT COURT

BRETT GENERAL CONTRACTING, LLC, a Nita corporation, Plaintiff, v. THE SCHOOL BOARD OF NITA COUNTY, Defendant.	CASE NO. 2-31869(12)(B)

DEFENDANT, THE SCHOOL BOARD OF NITA COUNTY'S, ANSWER AND AFFIRMATIVE DEFENSES AND COUNTERCLAIM TO PLAINTIFF, BRETT GENERAL CONTRACTING, LLC'S, COMPLAINT

Defendant, THE SCHOOL BOARD OF NITA COUNTY ("SBNC" or "owner"), by and through its undersigned counsel, hereby files its Answer and Affirmative Defenses and Counterclaim in response to Plaintiff, BRETT GENERAL CONTRACTING, LLC's ("BRETT"), Complaint.

I. ANSWER

GENERAL ALLEGATIONS

1. Without knowledge and therefore Denied.
2. Without knowledge and therefore Denied.
3. Admitted.
4. Admitted.
5. Admitted.
6. Admitted.
7. Denied.
8. Denied.
9. Denied.
10. Denied.
11. Denied.
12. Denied.
13. Denied.

COUNT I

14. SBNC readopts and re-alleges the answers to paragraphs 1 through 13 as though fully set forth herein.

15. Denied.

16. Denied.

COUNT II

17. SBNC readopts and re-alleges the answers to paragraphs 1 through 16 as though fully set forth herein.

18. Denied.

19. Denied.

II. AFFIRMATIVE DEFENSES

FIRST AFFIRMATIVE DEFENSE UNCLEAN HANDS

20. BRETT comes before this court with unclean hands. In furtherance of this defense, SBNC asserts, without limitation, that BRETT has willfully brought frivolous and unsupported claims against SBNC and is seeking damages known to be unsupported, unavailable, precluded by the parties' contract, or clearly excessive. Specifically, BRETT has willfully failed to comply with the various notice and claim procedures of the parties' contract, including the requirement that all change orders be in writing and executed by the contractor and owner before claims for additional compensation will be allowed. Additionally, to the extent that properly executed change orders do exist, the contract expressly provides that by executing a change order, BRETT waives and forever releases any claim against SBNC for additional time or compensation for issues or matters relating to or arising out of or resulting from the work included within or affected by the executed change order. Further, BRETT has breached the contract by charging excessive amounts, charging for amounts that are not authorized by the contract, and failing to complete its work within the time required by the contract.

SECOND AFFIRMATIVE DEFENSE SETOFF AND RECOUPMENT

21. BRETT's claim for damages is barred, in whole or in part, by the related doctrines of set-off and recoupment. Specifically, BRETT has breached the contract by charging excessive amounts, charging for amounts that are not authorized by the contract, and failing to complete its work within the time required by the contract. As a consequence, SBNC has overpaid BRETT amounts it was not due. Further, SBNC has incurred, or will incur, additional expenses and has sustained liquidated damages due to BRETT'S

delay in completing its required work. Specific examples of excessive or unauthorized charges include, but are not limited to, extended general conditions, labor/material costs, additional site supervision, working project manager/foreman costs, extended insurance costs, demobilization, and remobilization. As a result of the above, SBNC is entitled to a set-off against BRETT's damages, if any, or to otherwise recoup its own expenses incurred as a result of BRETT's actions.

THIRD AFFIRMATIVE DEFENSE
ESTOPPEL

22. BRETT's claims are barred, in whole or in part, by the doctrine of estoppel. Specifically, BRETT willingly, expressly, and unequivocally entered into a contract that expressly states that BRETT shall not be entitled to any claims for damages on account of hindrance or delays from any cause whatsoever, but if caused by any Act of God or active interference on the part of the owner, such action, hindrance, or delay may only entitle the contractor to receive an extension of time as its sole and exclusive remedy. Additionally, the contract contains explicit notice and claim requirements, including the requirement that all change orders be in writing and executed by the contractor and owner before claims for additional compensation will be allowed. Further, to the extent that properly executed change orders do exist, the contract expressly provides that by executing a change order, BRETT waives and forever releases any claim against SBNC for additional time or compensation for issues or matters relating to or arising out of or resulting from the work included within or affected by the executed change order. Since BRETT's entire claim for damages is based on delay, and the contract bars recovery for damages relating to delay, and BRETT utterly failed to comply with its contractual notice and claim requirements, BRETT is estopped from bringing this cause of action against SBNC.

FOURTH AFFIRMATIVE DEFENSE
WAIVER

23. BRETT's claims are barred, in whole or in part, by the doctrine of waiver. Specifically, BRETT willingly, expressly, and unequivocally entered into a contract that contains explicit notice and claim requirements, including the requirement that all change orders be in writing and executed by the contractor and owner before claims for additional compensation will be allowed. The contract clearly establishes that strict compliance with the notice and claim requirements is a condition precedent to any claim by BRETT for delay damages and that any failure of any condition precedent to occur shall constitute a complete waiver by BRETT of any claim for additional compensation. Additionally, to the extent that properly executed change orders do exist, the contract expressly provides that by executing a change order, BRETT waives and forever releases any claim against SBNC for additional time or compensation for issues or matters relating to, arising out of, or resulting from the work included within or affected by the executed change order. Finally, the contract expressly and unequivocally states BRETT shall not be entitled to any claims for damages on account of hindrance or delays from any cause whatsoever,

but if caused by any Act of God or active interference on the part of the owner, such action, hindrance, or delay may only entitle the contractor to receive an extension of time as its sole and exclusive remedy. Since BRETT's entire claim for damages is based on delay, the contract bars recovery for damages relating to delay, and BRETT utterly failed to comply with its contractual notice and claim requirements, BRETT is estopped from bringing this cause of action against SBNC.

SIXTH AFFIRMATIVE DEFENSE
FAILURE TO COMPLY WITH CONDITIONS PRECEDENT

24. BRETT's claims are barred, in whole or in part, because it failed to comply with all conditions precedent to bringing this action. Specifically, the contract contains detailed notice and claim provisions that must be complied with before any claim can be made by BRETT against SBNC. Additionally, the contracts require all change orders to be in writing and executed by the contractor and owner before claims for additional compensation will be allowed. BRETT has utterly failed to comply with any of these conditions precedent, and as such, the claims asserted in its complaint are waived and barred.

SEVENTH AFFIRMATIVE DEFENSE
FAILURE TO STATE A CAUSE OF ACTION FOR BREACH OF CONTRACT

25. BRETT's complaint fails to state a cause of action for breach of contract. Specifically, the complaint fails to allege the factual basis by which SBNC has waived sovereign immunity for BRETT's alleged claims, fails to allege compliance with the required contractual notice and claim procedures, fails to specifically allege, or even refer to, what change orders form the basis of its claims, fails to identify any express contractual provision which has been allegedly breached by SBNC, and fails to attach all required documents to its complaint in violation of N. R. Civ. P. 14.130(a).

EIGHTH AFFIRMATIVE DEFENSE
SOVEREIGN IMMUNITY

26. BRETT's claims are barred, in whole or in part, by the doctrine of sovereign immunity. As a matter of law, BRETT is not entitled to recover any damages for additional sums above the amount specified within the lump sum contract in the absence of a duly executed written change order approved by SBNC. Additionally, under Nita law, the doctrine of sovereign immunity bars recovery for damages where a contractor's claim is not supported by the contract provisions entered into between the parties because of failure by the contractor to follow the contract claims procedure contained therein. BRETT does not have an executed change order approved by SBNC and did not comply with any of the required contractual claims procedures. As such, BRETT's claim is barred in its entirety as a matter of law.

NINTH AFFIRMATIVE DEFENSE
NO DAMAGE FOR DELAY

27. BRETT's claims are barred, in whole or in part, by the no-damages-for-delay clause contained in the contract. BRETT's complaint seeks delay damages resulting from the alleged delay in completion of the project caused by SBNC or SBNC's project architects. The contractual provisions voluntarily entered into between the parties expressly and explicitly preclude recovery of the damages sought by BRETT. The contract expressly states BRETT shall not be entitled to any claims for damages on account of hindrance or delays from any cause whatsoever. Damages caused by any Act of God or active interference on the part of the owner, such as action, hindrance, or delay, may only entitle the contractor to receive an extension of time as its sole and exclusive remedy. Since BRETT's entire claim for damages is based on delay, the contractual provisions and law of the case bar BRETT from bringing this cause of action against SBNC.

COUNTERCLAIM

COMES NOW the Defendant/Third-Party Plaintiff/Counter-Plaintiff, THE SCHOOL BOARD OF NITA COUNTY ("SBNC"), by and through its undersigned counsel, and sues Plaintiff/Counter-Defendant, BRETT GENERAL CONTRACTING, LLC ("BRETT"), by alleging:

GENERAL ALLEGATIONS

1. This is an action for damages in excess of $15,000.00, exclusive of interest, costs, and attorneys' fees.
2. The SBNC is a political subdivision of the State of Nita and located in Nita County, Nita.
3. BRETT is a Nita for-profit corporation authorized to do business in the state of Nita and has its principal place of business in Nita County, Nita.
4. Venue is proper in this court pursuant to Section 47.011, Nita Statutes, as the subject matter of the alleged claims arise out of a contract for the design of improvements to real property located in Nita County, Nita, and all alleged causes of action arose in Nita County, Nita.
5. On or about March 10, YR-3, SBNC and BRETT entered into a contract for construction services ("contract") for the construction of a cafeteria and eight classrooms in the Alan B. Whitfield Elementary School. A true and correct copy of the contract is attached and incorporated into this counterclaim as Exhibit A.

COUNT I. BREACH OF CONTRACT

6. SBNC realleges the allegations of paragraphs 1–5.
7. As a direct and proximate result of BRETT's failure to perform its contractual duties as set forth below, BRETT materially breached the contract by, among other things:

a. Charging excessive amounts and amounts not authorized by the contract, including but not limited to extended general conditions, labor/material costs, additional site supervision, working project manager/foreman costs, extended insurance costs, demobilization, and remobilization. BRETT's excessive and unauthorized charges damaged SBNC by causing it to overpay BRETT;

b. Failing to comply with the various notice and claim procedures of the contract, including the requirement that all change orders be in writing and executed by the contractor and owner before claims for additional compensation will be allowed; and

c. Delaying the project, causing damages to SBNC, and subjecting BRETT to liquidated damages;

8. In particular, BRETT materially breached the following provisions in its contract with SBNC, in addition to other breaches that may be revealed as discovery progresses in this case:

   a. Failing to provide SBNC with notice, in writing, of the cause of any hindrance or delay after its occurrence in violation of the contract;

   b. Charging excessive or unauthorized amounts in violation of the general conditions of the contract;

   c. Failing to comply with the requirement that all change orders be in writing and executed by the contractor and owner before claims for additional compensation will be allowed, in violation of the general conditions of the contract; and

   d. Failing to complete its work within the time required by the contract, resulting in a significant delay in reaching substantial completion of the project in violation of the contract, and a further delay in obtaining final completion of the project in violation of the contract, for which SBNC is entitled to recover liquidated damages against BRETT pursuant to the contract.

9. As a direct and proximate result of BRETT'S above described material breaches of the contract, SBNC has suffered, and continues to suffer, damages in an amount in excess of $15,000.00.

10. All of the conditions precedent to this action have occurred, have been performed, have been waived, or otherwise excused.

CERTIFICATE OF SERVICE

I HEREBY CERTIFY that a true and correct copy of the foregoing has been furnished via email pursuant to Nita Rule of Judicial Administration 4.200 to Ernie Bock, Jr., Esquire, Bock, Bock & Associates, 1251 Main Street, Suite 2500, Nita City, Nita 57818 on this 15th day of December, YR-2.

STEWART LAW, PA
Attorneys for Defendant
432 Hill Street
Nita City, Nita 57818
(819) 555-1560 – Telephone
(819) 555-7800 – Facsimile

By: /s/ Marsha Stewart
Marsha Stewart, Esq.
Nita Bar No. 41832

IN THE STATE OF NITA
NITA COUNTY CIRCUIT COURT

BRETT GENERAL CONTRACTING, LLC, a Nita corporation, Plaintiff, v. THE SCHOOL BOARD OF NITA COUNTY, Defendant.	CASE NO. 2-31869(12)(B)

PLAINTIFF, BRETT GENERAL CONTRACTING, LLC'S, ANSWER TO DEFENDANT, THE SCHOOL BOARD OF NITA COUNTY'S, COUNTERCLAIM

Plaintiff, BRETT GENERAL CONTRACTING, LLC's ("BRETT"), by and through its undersigned counsel, hereby files its Answer in response to Defendant, THE SCHOOL BOARD OF NITA COUNTY's ("SBNC"), Counterclaim.

ANSWER
GENERAL ALLEGATIONS

1. Admitted
2. Admitted.
3. Admitted.
4. Admitted.
5. Admitted.

COUNT I
BREACH OF CONTRACT

6. Admitted.
7. Denied, all parts.
8. Denied, all parts.
9. Denied.
10. Denied.

CERTIFICATE OF SERVICE

I HEREBY CERTIFY that a true and correct copy of the foregoing has been furnished via email pursuant to Nita Rule of Judicial Administration 4.200 to Marsha Stewart, Esquire, Stewart Law, PA, 432 Hill Street, Nita City, Nita 57818 on this 29th day of December, YR-2.

LAW OFFICES
BOCK, BOCK, & ASSOCIATES
ATTORNEYS FOR PLAINTIFF
1251 Main Street, Suite 2500
Nita City, Nita 57818
(819) 555-1200 – Telephone
(819) 555-7800 – Facsimile

By: /s/ Ernie Bock
Ernie Bock, Jr., Esq.
Nita Bar No. 092893

Jury Instructions

Jury Instruction #1: Members of the jury, I shall now instruct you on the law that you must follow in reaching your verdicts. It is your duty to render a verdict only on the issues that I submit for your determination. You must consider and weigh the evidence, resolve the disputed issues of fact, and apply the law as I instruct you to facts as you find them from the evidence. The evidence consists of the sworn testimony of witnesses, all exhibits received in evidence, all facts stipulated or agreed upon by the parties, and any fact of which the court has taken judicial notice. In determining the facts, you may draw reasonable inferences from the evidence. You may make deductions and reach conclusions that reason and common sense support. However, you must not speculate on matters outside the admitted evidence.

Jury Instruction #2: You will hear me use the term "greater weight of the evidence" throughout these instructions. Greater weight of the evidence means the more persuasive and convincing force and effect of the entire evidence in this case.

Jury Instruction #3: Your duty as jurors is to decide the issues that I submit for your determination and communicate your determination by answering the questions on the verdict form. You must come to an agreement about your verdict. Your agreed upon answers to my questions are called your jury verdict. The evidence in this case consists of the sworn testimony of the witnesses, all exhibits received in evidence, and all facts that were admitted or agreed to by the parties. In reaching your verdict, you must think about and weigh the testimony and any documents, photographs, or other material received in evidence. You may also consider any facts admitted or agreed to by the lawyers. Your job is to determine what the facts are. You may use reason and common sense to reach conclusions. You may draw reasonable inferences from the evidence, but you should not guess about things that were not covered here. You must always apply the law as I will explain it to you.

Jury Instruction #4: In evaluating the believability of any witness and the weight you will give the testimony of any witness, you may consider the demeanor of the witness while testifying, the frankness or a lack of frankness of the witness, as well as any interest the witness may have in the outcome of the case. Consider also the means and opportunity the witness had to know the facts about which they testified, the witness's ability to remember the matters about which they testified, and the reasonableness of their testimony in light of all the evidence in the case and in light of your own experience and common sense.

[**Expert witnesses.** You have heard opinion testimony on certain technical subjects from people referred to as expert witnesses. Some of the testimony before you was in the form of opinions about certain technical subjects. You may accept this opinion testimony, reject it, or give it the weight you think it deserves considering the knowledge, skill, experience, training, or education of the witness, the reasons given by the witness for the opinion expressed, and all the other evidence in this case.]

Jury Instruction #5: The case before you is a contract dispute between Brett General Contracting and the School Board of Nita County. A contract is an agreement between parties, creating mutual obligations that are enforceable by law. Contracts consist of many agreements that are known as clauses. Every contract clause imposes on each of the parties an implied obligation of good faith, cooperation, and fair dealing in its performance. Contract clauses aimed at relieving a party from some consequences of its own fault are disfavored in the law.

Jury Instruction #6: The parties agree that on or about March 10, YR-3, they entered into a contract for Brett Contracting to perform construction services, including furnishing labor and materials, for renovations to the Alan B. Whitfield Elementary School. The plans for the renovations were drawn up by Sonia Forester, an architect with We Build Nita, Inc. The architect is the agent of the School Board of Nita County. This means that the architect was hired by and was responsible to the school board throughout the project.

The parties also agree that during the course of construction, numerous problems arose in connection with the build design plans provided to Brett General Contracting. These problems caused completion of the project to be delayed.

Jury Instruction #7: The issues for your determination are as follows: 1) whether the School Board of Nita County acted in bad faith and materially breached the agreement with Brett General Contracting by failing to compensate Brett General Contracting for its work, or 2) whether Brett General Contracting instead materially breached its contract with the School Board of Nita County by charging unauthorized and excessive costs in excess of the contract. I will talk about Brett General Contracting's claims first.

Jury Instruction #8: Brett General Contracting claims the School Board of Nita County acted in bad faith by breaching its implied duty not to hinder or impede the performance of its work and that the breach resulted in damages to Brett General Contracting. To constitute material breach of contract, a party's nonperformance of an obligation must go to the very essence of the contract. In other words, the School Board of Nita County's failure to perform some minor part of its contractual obligation would not constitute a material breach, nor would it excuse Brett General Contracting from performing its contractual obligations. In deciding whether the School Board of Nita County acted in bad faith and breached the contract, you must determine from the greater weight of the evidence if the School Board of Nita County failed to substantially perform under the contract.

Jury Instruction #9: As I said, contracts consist of many agreements that are known as clauses. One of the clauses in this contract is called a no-damages-for-delay clause. A no-damages-for-delay clause is enforceable except when bad faith occurs. Bad faith is defined as the opposite of good faith, generally implying or involving actual or constructive fraud, behavior designed to mislead or deceive another, fraudulently operating or managing a business or other entity, or some motive of interest or ill will. A complete catalog of the types of bad faith is impossible, but among the types that have been recognized is interference with or failure to cooperate in the other party's performance.

Mere negligence or lack of diligence will not support a finding of bad faith. Mere lethargy is also not considered bad faith and will not overcome a no-damages-for-delay clause.

The no-damages-for-delay clause in this contract reads as follows:

> The contractor shall not be entitled to any claim for damages time on account of hindrance or delays from any cause whatsoever. However, if a delay is caused by an Act of God or active interference on part of the owner, such act, hinderance, or delay may only entitle the contractor to receive an extension of time as its sole and exclusive remedy. . . . The contractor recognizes and specifically acknowledges the terms and conditions of the "no damage for delay" clause upon execution of this contract.

In order to avoid this no-damages-for-delay clause on the basis of bad faith, Brett General Contracting must prove that the School Board of Nita County engaged in bad faith conduct that materially impaired Brett General Contracting's ability to timely complete the project. If you find that the delay Brett General Contracting complains of was caused by the School Board of Nita County's bad faith, then the no-damages-for-delay clause will be of no effect and Brett General Contracting will be entitled to recover the damages it proves to you by the greater weight of the evidence; otherwise, you may not permit Brett General Contracting to recover any damages on account of any delay in completion of the construction project.

Jury Instruction #10: If you find by greater weight of the evidence that the School Board of Nita County engaged in bad faith, making the no-damages-for-delay clause unenforceable, you must next determine the damages that Brett General Contracting is entitled to recover for the project delays based upon the evidence, the rules of law in which I instruct you, and the other instructions that I will give you on the subject of damages. The damages you award must be supported by evidence justifying the definite amount, not speculation. Damages must be proven with reasonable certainty.

Jury Instruction #11: A party injured by another's breach of contract has a duty to take all reasonable steps to protect itself and to mitigate or diminish its damages. Upon becoming aware of a breach, the non-breaching party must act reasonably to minimize any resulting loss or harm and may not recover damages for losses or harm that could have been avoided through reasonable efforts or expenditures. If you find from the greater weight of the evidence that Brett General Contracting could have avoided all or part of the damages it claims by making reasonable efforts or expenditures after learning of a breach, you should reduce the damages you award to Brett General Contracting to account for any loss or harm that could have reasonably avoided.

Jury Instruction #12: The School Board of Nita County has raised several affirmative defenses. In an affirmative defense, the defendant introduces evidence that, if found to be credible, will negate civil liability, even if it is proven that the defendant committed the alleged acts. Each of these defenses has its own set of elements that the defendant must establish in order for the affirmative defense to prevail. I will now explain these defenses.

> **Jury Instruction #12A:** The School Board of Nita County has raised the defense of sovereign immunity. State entities such as the School Board of Nita County are protected by sovereign immunity under Nita law. The doctrine of sovereign immunity precludes recovery of damages for extra work performed under a construction contract unless the additional costs claimed were addressed in the original contract or in a subsequent modification to the contract (a written and executed change order).
>
> When the extra work claimed is outside the terms of the contract and the claimant did not obtain a duly authorized written modification of the contract, such a claim for extra work is not valid. Therefore, if you find by the greater weight of the evidence that the compensation Brett General Contracting claims was for extra work that was outside the terms of the original contract and authorized written modifications, or if you find that Brett General Contracting did not properly follow the contractual notification procedure, then you must enter a verdict against Brett General Contracting and in favor of the School Board of Nita County.
>
> **Jury Instruction #12B:** The School Board of Nita County has raised the defense of waiver. A waiver is a voluntary and intentional relinquishment of a known right. A waiver can either be made by an expressed statement or implied by conduct, acts, or circumstances surrounding the parties that leads one party to believe that a known right has been waived. If you find

that Brett General Contracting's asserted right to additional compensation has been waived, the School Board of Nita County must establish each of the following elements by the greater weight of the evidence: 1) the existence of the right, privilege, advantage, or benefit that may be waived; 2) the actual or constructive knowledge of the right, privilege, advantage, or benefit; and 3) an intention to relinquish that right, privilege, advantage, or benefit. If the greater weight of the evidence establishes these three factors, your verdict should be for the School Board of Nita County. If, however, the greater weight of the evidence does not support the defense of the School Board of Nita County, you shall consider the other affirmative defenses.

Jury Instruction #12C: An additional defense for the school board is whether Brett General Contracting is estopped from asserting its demand for additional compensation. The doctrine of equitable estoppel is based on notions of fair play and essential justice. Estoppel arises when one party lulls another party into a disadvantaged legal position. The representation upon which an estoppel may be predicated consists of words, conduct, or, if there is a duty to speak, silence. To find that Brett General Contracting is estopped from demanding additional compensation, the School Board of Nita County must establish the following elements by the greater weight of the evidence: 1) that Brett General Contracting represented a material fact that is contrary to a later asserted position; 2) that the School Board of Nita County relied on that representation; and 3) that a change in the representation and reliance was detrimental to the School Board of Nita County. If the greater weight of the evidence supports the defense of the School Board of Nita County on this issue, your verdict should be for the School Board of Nita County. If, however, the greater weight of the evidence does not support this defense, you shall consider the other affirmative defenses.

Jury Instruction #13: I will now address the school board's counterclaim. The School Board of Nita County has asserted a counterclaim against Brett General Contracting for breach of contract. The School Board of Nita County claims that Brett General Contracting breached the party's contract in some or all of the following ways: A) charging excessive amounts and amounts not authorized by the contract; B) failing to comply with the various notice and claim procedures of the contract; C) failing to provide all required critical path analyses, dollar value graphs, time graphs, and other required schedules and supporting documentations; D) failing to comply with the requirements that all change orders be in writing and executed by the contractor and owner before claims for additional compensation will be allowed; and E) failing to complete its work within the time required by the contract. As a result of these breaches, the School Board of Nita County contends that it has sustained and continues to suffer monetary losses.

Jury Instruction #14: To recover damages from Brett General Contracting for breach of contract, the School Board of Nita County must prove each of the following by the greater weight of the evidence: 1) the School Board of Nita County and Brett General Contracting entered into a contract; 2) that Brett General Contracting failed to do something that the contract required it to do, and 3) that the School Board of Nita County was harmed by that failure. The parties do not dispute the first element, the existence of a valid written contract. Therefore, the success or failure of the School Board of Nita County's breach of contract counterclaim will depend on satisfying the second and third elements, whether Brett General Contracting failed to perform any one or more of its obligations on the contract and, if so, whether the School Board of Nita County was damaged by such failure and by how much.

Jury Instruction #15: To constitute material breach of contract, the party's nonperformance of an obligation must go to the very essence of the contract. Thus, Brett General Contracting's failure to perform some minor part of its contractual obligations does not constitute material breach nor does it excuse the School Board of Nita County's performance under the contract. In deciding whether Brett General Contracting breached its contract, you must determine from the greater weight of the evidence if Brett General Contracting failed to substantially perform under the contract.

Therefore, if you find by the greater weight of the evidence that Brett General Contracting failed to substantially perform its obligations under the contract by A) charging excessive amounts and amounts not authorized by the contract; B) failing to comply with any of the notice and claim procedures of the contract; C) failing to provide all required critical path analyses, dollar value graphs, time graphs, and other required schedules and supporting documentation; D) failing to comply with the requirement that all change orders be in writing and executed by the owner before claims for additional compensation will be allowed; or E) failing to complete its work within the time required by the contract; then you must find in favor of the School Board of Nita County on its breach of contract counterclaim and determine the amount, if any, by which the School Board of Nita County has been damaged by each of the Brett General Contracting breaches.

Jury Instruction #16: If you find that Brett General Contracting materially breached the contract that they made with the School Board of Nita County, you must award the School Board of Nita County damages for that breach. You must determine the amount of damages to be awarded based upon the evidence, the rules of the law on which I have instructed you, and all the other instructions that I will give you on the subject of damages.

Jury Instruction #17: The School Board of Nita County has the same duty to take all reasonable steps to protect itself and to mitigate or diminish its damages as discussed previously. Upon becoming aware of a breach, the non-breaching party must act reasonably to minimize any resulting loss or harm and may not recover damages for losses or harm that could have been avoided through reasonable efforts or expenditures. If you find from the greater weight of the evidence that the School Board of Nita County could have avoided all or part of the damages it claims by making reasonable efforts or expenditures after learning of a breach, you should reduce the damages you award to the School Board of Nita County to account for any loss or harm it could have reasonably avoided.

Jury Instruction #18: Members of the jury, you have now heard all the evidence, my instructions on the law that you must apply in reaching your verdict, and the closing arguments of the attorneys. You will shortly retire to the jury room to decide this case. Before you do so, I have a few last instructions for you. During deliberations, jurors must communicate about the case only with one another and only when all jurors are present in the jury room. You will have in the jury room all of the evidence that was received during the trial. In reaching your decision, do not do any research on your own or as a group. Do not use dictionaries, the internet, or any other reference materials. Do not investigate the case or conduct any experiments. Do not visit or view the scene of any event involved in this case or look at maps or pictures on the internet.

If you happen to pass by the scene, do not stop or investigate. All jurors must see or hear the same evidence at the same time. Do not read, listen to, or watch any news accounts of this trial. You are not to communicate with any person outside of the jury about this case. Until you have reached your verdict, you must not talk about this case in person or through the telephone, in writing, or by electronic communications such as a blog, social media account, email, text message, or any other means. Do not contact anyone to assist you such as a family accountant, doctor, or lawyer.

These communication rules apply until I have discharged you at the end of the case. If you become aware of any violation of these instructions or any other instruction that I have given in this case, you must tell me by giving a note to the bailiff. Any notes that you have taken during this trial may be taken to the jury room for use during your discussions. Your notes are simply an aid to your own memory and neither your notes nor those of any other juror are binding or conclusive. Your notes are not a substitute for your own memory or that of other jurors. Instead, your verdict must result from the collective memory and judgment of all jurors based on the evidence and testimony presented during the trial. At the conclusion of the trial, the bailiff will collect your notes, which will be immediately destroyed. No one will ever read your notes after the conclusion of this trial.

In reaching your verdict, do not let bias, sympathy, prejudice, public opinion, or any other sentiment for or against any party influence your decision. Your verdict must be based on the evidence that has been received and the law on which I have instructed you. Reaching a verdict is exclusively your job. I cannot participate in that decision in any way, and you should not guess what I think your verdict should be from something I may have said or done. You should not think that I prefer one verdict over another. Therefore, in reaching your verdict you should not consider anything that I have said or done except for my specific instructions to you. Pay careful attention to all the instructions that I gave you, for that is the law that you must follow.

You will have a copy of my instructions with you when you go to the jury room to deliberate. All the instructions are important, and you must consider all of them together. There are no other laws that apply to this case, and even if you do not agree with these laws, you must use them in reaching your decision in this case.

When you go to the jury room, the first thing you should do is choose a presiding juror to act as a foreperson during your deliberations. The foreperson should see to it that your discussions are orderly and that everyone has a fair chance to be heard. It is your duty to talk with one another in the jury room and to consider the views of all the jurors. Each of you must decide the case for yourself, but only after you have considered the evidence with the other members of the jury.

Feel free to change your mind if you are convinced that your position should be different. You should all try to agree, but do not give up your honest beliefs just because the others think differently. Keep an open mind so that you and your fellow jurors can easily share ideas about the case. I will give you a verdict form with questions you must answer. I have already instructed you on the law that you are to use in answering these questions. You must follow my questions on the form carefully. You must consider each question separately. Please answer questions in the order that they appear and after you answer the question, the form tells you what to do next.

Your verdict must be unanimous; that is, your verdict must be agreed to by all of you. When you have agreed on your verdict and finished filling out the form, your foreperson must write the date and sign it at the bottom and return the verdict to the bailiff. If any of you need to communicate with me for any reason, write me a note and give it to the bailiff. In your note, do not disclose any vote or split or the reason for the communication.

IN THE STATE OF NITA
NITA COUNTY CIRCUIT COURT

BRETT GENERAL CONTRACTING, LLC, a Nita corporation, Plaintiff, v. THE SCHOOL BOARD OF NITA COUNTY, Defendant.	CASE NO. 2-31869(12)(B)

VERDICT FORM

WE, THE JURY, return the following verdict:

1. Do you find, from the greater weight of the evidence, that the SCHOOL BOARD OF NITA COUNTY acted in bad faith and breached the contract with BRETT GENERAL CONTRACTING?

______ YES ______ NO

If you answered YES to Question No. 1, then please proceed to Question No. 2. If you answered NO to Question No. 1, then please proceed to Question No. 3.

2. What, if any, is the amount of damages of BRETT GENERAL CONTRACTING'S claim that they are entitled to recover in this proceeding against THE SCHOOL BOARD OF NITA COUNTY?

$ ______________________________

3. As to THE SCHOOL BOARD OF NITA COUNTY's claim for breach of contract against BRETT GENERAL CONTRACTING, do you find that BRETT GENERAL CONTRACTING breached its contract?

______ YES ______ NO

If you answered YES to Question No. 3, please proceed to Question No. 4.

4. What is the amount of damages THE SCHOOL BOARD OF NITA COUNTY is entitled to recover from BRETT GENERAL CONTRACTING in this proceeding?

$ ______________________________

Please sign and return this verdict form.

Dated: ______________________ Foreperson: ____________________________

Signature

Depositions

IN THE STATE OF NITA
NITA COUNTY CIRCUIT COURT

BRETT GENERAL CONTRACTING, LLC, a Nita corporation,

Plaintiff,

v.

THE SCHOOL BOARD OF NITA COUNTY,

Defendant.

CASE NO. 2-31869(12)(B)

VIDEO DEPOSITION OF RICHARD BRETT

April 2, YR-1

9:30 a.m.

Remote Proceeding
Nita City, Nita

DANIEL PEREZ
Digital Reporter
Commission No. NN 389855

APPEARANCES OF COUNSEL

On behalf of Plaintiff, Brett General Contracting, LLC:

ERNIE BOCK, JR., ESQ.
BOCK, BOCK & ASSOCIATES
1251 Main Street
Suite 2500
Nita City, Nita 57818
APPEARED VIA VIDEOCONFERENCE

On behalf of Defendant, the School Board of Nita County:

MARSHA STEWART, ESQ.
STEWART LAW, P.A.
432 Hill Street
Nita City, Nita 57818
APPEARED VIA VIDEOCONFERENCE

Also Present:
Jordan McHugh, Videographer

INDEX TO EXAMINATION

INDEX OF EXHIBITS

[Exhibits 1 through 10 were attached to the original transcript.]

THE VIDEOGRAPHER: Good morning. We are now on the record. The time is 9:30 a.m. on Saturday, April 2, YR-1. This begins the videotaped deposition of Richard Brett, taken in the matter of Brett General Contracting versus the School Board of Nita County filed in the Circuit Court of the 10th Judicial Circuit in and for Nita County, Nita; case number 2-31869(12)(B).

The videographer today is Jordan McHugh. The court reporter today is Daniel Perez. We are both representing eScribe Transcriptions.

Counsel, will you please announce your name and whom you represent, after which the court reporter will swear in our witness.

MR. BOCK: Ernie Bock, Jr., representing plaintiff.

MS. STEWART: Marsha Stewart, representing the defendant.

THE REPORTER: Good morning, everyone. My name is Daniel Perez, Notary Public and digital reporter for eScribe Transcriptions in the state of Nita. The witness is currently located in Nita City, Nita, and has confirmed his identity by driver's license.

Absent any objections at this time, counsel

and the witness agree to my remote administration of the oath to the witness and that the final transcript may be used for all purposes allowed by local rules of civil procedure.

Hearing no objections, this shall constitute agreement and stipulation of such and I will now swear in the witness.

Mr. Brett, please raise your right hand to be sworn.

RICHARD BRETT,

having first been duly sworn, testified as follows:

THE WITNESS: Yes, ma'am. I do.

THE REPORTER: Okay. Counsel, you may begin.

MS. STEWART: Thank you.

EXAMINATION

BY MS. STEWART:

Q. Good morning, Mr. Brett.

A. Morning.

Q. My name is Marsha Stewart and I represent the defendant in this matter, School Board of Nita County.

A. Yes, ma'am. I know who you are.

Q. You understand that you are under oath and that being under oath means you are sworn to tell the truth?

A. Yes.

Q. Have you ever had your deposition taken in the past?
A. Yes.
Q. And you understand that your responses here have the same force as in a courtroom with a judge and jury?
A. Yes.
Q. Are you prepared to answer my questions today?
A. Yes, ma'am.
Q. Okay. Is there anything that will prevent you from providing me with your full attention?
A. No, ma'am.
Q. You haven't taken any medication that'll alter your ability to answer the questions today?
A. No, ma'am.
Q. Will you let me know if you don't understand one of my questions?
A. Yes, ma'am.
Q. If you need to take a break at any time, just tell me; we'll take a break. Is that okay?
A. Yes.
Q. Okay. What is your full name?
A. Richard Brett.
Q. Have you ever used any other names?
A. No.

Q. Do you have any nicknames?
A. Nope.
Q. What is your date of birth and where were you born?
A. January 19, YR-52, in Nita City.
Q. Okay. What does that make your age?
A. 52.
Q. And what is your current address?
A. 21 Chelsea Court, Nita City, Nita 57819.
Q. Do you have any licenses or certifications?
A. Yes. I have a GC, a general contractor's license.
Q. Okay. Have you ever been arrested?
A. No.
Q. Ever been convicted of a crime?
A. No, ma'am.
Q. Have you been involved in any other legal claims or lawsuits?
A. Yes. Seems like people are always suing general contractors.
Q. What was the outcome of your prior lawsuits?
A. It was dismissed as frivolous.
Q. How did you prepare for this deposition today?
A. I didn't.
Q. You didn't even meet with your counsel?

A. No, ma'am.
Q. Mr. Brett, where are you employed?
A. I currently own my own contracting business.
Q. Now, let's turn to the contract you signed with the School Board of Nita County on March 10, YR-3. I'm going to show you a contract.
Is this the contract you signed with the School Board of Nita County to renovate eight classrooms and expand the cafeteria at Alan B. Whitfield Elementary School?
A. Yes, ma'am, this is it.
MS. STEWART: Okay. Let's mark this contract into evidence as Exhibit No. 1.
(Exhibit 1 was marked for identification.)
BY MS. STEWART:
Q. Mr. Brett, please take a look at Exhibit 1. What's the address of that school project?
A. 1532 Nita Road, Nita City, Nita 57818.
Q. Mr. Brett, do you consider yourself a sophisticated businessman?
A. I do.
Q. Did you read this contract before you signed it?
A. Pretty much. Maybe not every word, especially because I previously signed other contracts with the

School Board of Nita County, and I assumed this was the same.

Q. So, you were aware that this contract had specific requirements for submitting any changes to the project that would affect the cost or time for completion of the project?

A. Yes, ma'am. But on prior projects, I've worked closely with the project managers on the projects. We call them PMs. And getting paid was not so formal with submittals having to be approved by the school board.

Q. Can you explain that a little further?

A. Sure. On prior projects, I could simply call or email the PM I was working with on the projects, and they would sign off on changes and approve payments to me.

Q. If you reviewed the contract, you were also aware that there was a no-damages-for-delay clause included in the contract, correct?

A. Yes, I believe that's in all their contracts. But, again, I've never had a problem getting paid in full on my previous projects.

Q. Were any of the school board—prior school board projects for the same or similar remodels?

A. Yes, ma'am.

Q. Did you rely on the same or similar architectural plans for these prior school remodels?

A. Yes. In fact, one project was for the exact same classroom and cafeteria addition. The drawings were the same for that project. We incurred a few delays in that project as well, and I was paid by the School Board for those additional delays—delay costs on the project, which is why I didn't anticipate any issues with submitting my change orders for this project.

Q. Well, let me show you an invoice dated September 19, YR-4, where Brett General Contracting, LLC, which is you, submitted for payment on a prior job at the Nita Public High School. That project incurred delay costs but still has a "paid" stamp on it.

Is this the invoice for the prior project that you're referring to?

A. Just give me a minute to take a look. Yes. This is it. I was paid in full for that project. And that project, I'd also had a few delays, and I incurred some additional expenses that I was paid for. I—I paid out of pocket, but I was paid.

MS. STEWART: Let's have the court reporter mark this prior invoice dated September 19, YR-4, into the record as Exhibit 2, please.

(Exhibit 2 was marked for identification.)
BY MS. STEWART:
Q. Okay. Let's walk through the payment process on this project. You commenced work and submitted an initial change order with some minor modifications on April 22, YR-3, correct?
A. I—ma'am.
Q. Looking at this change order, is this the change order that you submitted on this project? Take your time.
A. Yes, it is. I—I submitted this change order to the project manager, Tom Smith. I submitted it to him directly.
MS. STEWART: And okay. Madam Court Reporter, can you please mark this change order dated April 22, YR-3 into evidence as Exhibit 3, please.
(Exhibit 3 was marked for identification.)
BY MS. STEWART:
Q. Mr. Brett, did you get paid in full for the modifications submitted to the School Board of Nita County outlined on this change order?
A. Yes, I did. And I received the payment almost immediately. No delay.
Q. Do you know whether the project manager submitted this initial change order to the school

board for approval?
A. I have no idea. I just know I got paid.
Q. Were there any other modifications to the project that affected your costs or delays in meeting the completion dates on this project?
A. Yes. Tom Smith, the initial project manager? He was out sick for long time, so we could not obtain responses from him. That was a problem when work shut down due to the pandemic. I asked Tom for an exemption because we were working outdoors. I called several times but he never got back to me. During this period, though, my company was still responsible for storage fees, payroll, equipment rentals, and other items. Our expenses didn't stop because Tom got sick.
Q. Did you submit another change order for these expenses and claim extensions?
A. I sure did. I submitted it multiple times. First to Tom, the first project manager, then I had to follow up and submit it several times to Carol Marks, the second project manager that came on board when Tom went out on disability.
Q. Take a look, please, at this email with its attachments, change order, and out of pocket expenses. Is this the second change order that you submitted on this project to Tom Smith?
A. Yep. Yes, it is.

MS. STEWART: We're going to now mark this June 24, YR-3, email submitting the second change order as Composite Exhibit 4, please.

(Exhibit 4 was marked for identification.)

BY MS. STEWART:

Q. Now, taking a look at Exhibit 4, this is where you submitted the second change order to the first project manager. Were you paid after submitting this change order?

A. No, but I did receive a voicemail from Tom. He said he was sorry for the delay. He said the delay was his fault, and he would make sure the change order was paid before he left on disability.

Q. He left a voicemail. Let's listen to this audio of that actual voicemail that you received from Tom Smith on July 6, YR-3.

A. Okay.

MS. STEWART: Give me one second. I'm going to play that.

THE WITNESS: It's always a delay on the school board's end. I have it here in my office if you want me to play it.

(Audio played.)

MS. STEWART: Let's mark this voicemail as Exhibit 5, please.

(Exhibit 5 was marked for identification.)
BY MS. STEWART:
Q. Did Tom get you paid before he left the project?
A. Well, that was the voicemail he left me. Just like I told you, he said that he'd pay me. That's the voicemail I received. But no. No, he—he didn't pay. I didn't get paid. I then had to send the second change order to the new project manager who came onto the project. I emailed Carol Marks a copy of the second change order on September 3rd—September 3, YR-3, telling her that Tom said it was approved for payment and asked her to get it paid.
MS. STEWART: Let's mark this email to Carol Marks you're talking about as Composite Exhibit 6.
(Exhibit 6 was marked for identification.)
BY MS. STEWART:
Q. Can you take a look at that, please?
A. Yes.
Q. What happened next? Were you paid?
A. No, I still haven't been paid. Carol stopped by the project on January 19, YR-2. I wasn't on the site that day, but Carol left me a handwritten note on my desk in the construction trailer, and she said she would see to it that I got paid.

Q. Take a look at this handwritten note. Is this the note that Carol left on your desk?

A. Yes.

Q. Looks like a—

A. Yeah, I see.

Q. Looks like a Post-it, doesn't it?

A. Yeah. That's exactly right. Rich FYI SBNC—that's you guys—said they'll pay the CO. Stay tuned. Well, I'm still tuned.

MS. STEWART: Well, please mark this handwritten note as Exhibit 7.

(Exhibit 7 was marked for identification.)

BY MS. STEWART:

Q. Now, did you get paid for that second change order?

A. Nope. That's when I received this letter from the school board advised me that they denied my request for payment of the second change order.

Q. Okay. I'm showing you now a February 22, YR-2, letter from the School Board of Nita County, board member Holly Williams. Is this the denial letter you were referring to?

A. Yes, ma'am. That's it.

MS. STEWART: Okay. We're going to mark this one—this letter as Exhibit 8, please.

(Exhibit 8 was marked for identification.)
BY MS. STEWART:
Q. Is this the letter, Exhibit 8, that the school board—did the school board say why in this letter the payment for the second change order was denied?
A. Yeah. According to the letter, they're saying that neither Tom nor Carol had the authority to approve payments for delays without—without the board approving. I don't know what happened before, but I always got paid and they handled it. Tom handled it.
This letter also says that my request for payment never even came up for the school board and that it was denied because the contract does not cover damages for delay, which is just BS if you ask me. I've been paid many, many times in the past for prior projects working for the school board where there were also delays, and I was paid on those.
On this project, I received confirmation from both the managers, Tom and that lady, both, Carol, the payment was approved. But now they are trying to pull this nonsense. You know, I did my part completing the project. I had no control over their employees being out sick, their delays doing—having to replace their project managers. I know that stuff happens, but it wasn't my problem, nor was the

pandemic. But I still haven't gotten paid.

BY MS. STEWART:

Q. Well, was the project completed on time?

A. The classroom remodel was completed on time, although there was a slight delay in completing the cafeteria expansion. Even though I had not been paid, I kept getting—I kept getting emails from the second project manager, that Carol lady, inquiring about the project's completion date.

She kept reminding me about the contract date for completing both projects prior to the next school year, which I was fully aware of. She didn't need to keep reminding me, especially when—especially when had it not been for the multiple project managers, lack of communication from the project managers, and the pandemic, the project would have been completed early.

Q. Let's take a look at this set of emails you're talking about. Are these the emails you received from the second project manager, Carol Marks, asking you about their project completion status?

A. Just have a look at these. Yeah. Carol's good at writing emails, not so good at writing checks. Yeah. These are the emails.

MS. STEWART: Let's mark these two emails

dated April 22, YR-2 and June 23, YR-2 as Composite Exhibit 9, please.

(Exhibit 9 was marked for identification.)

BY MS. STEWART:

Q. Now, did you ever finish the project?

A. Yes. I notified the school board's representative who is stipulated to receive notices. The person they said, you got to notice, you send it to this person. That's in the contract. And I sent the correspondence on two occasions. The first was a letter advising the classrooms have been completed, and the second letter advised them that the cafeteria was completed. So therefore, the entire project was now completed, and please provide final payment.

Q. So, you advised them. So, are these the two letters I'm showing you now that you sent advising the school board about the project completion?

A. Yeah. This is—these are my letters. You like the logo in the letterhead?

Q. Definitely a GC. Okay.

MS. STEWART: Let's mark these two letters dated June 20, YR-2 and August 17, YR-2 as Composite Exhibit 10, please.

(Exhibit 10 was marked for identification.)

BY MS. STEWART:

Q. Now, after all was said and done, you had completed the project entirely, were you ever paid in full?

A. No. That's why I had to file this lawsuit to get them to pay me.

Q. One last question. After wrapping up this particular renovation project for the School Board of Nita County, are you still working on new projects with the school board?

A. Yes, I am.

MS. STEWART: Counsel, I have no further questions, but we would like a copy of the transcript. Any questions on cross?

MR. BOCK: Yes. Just one. Hopefully just one.

EXAMINATION

BY MR. BOCK:

Q. Hello, Mr. Brett.

A. Morning.

Q. Were you paid everything you were owed on this project except for the delay costs in the second change order?

A. Yes. But as I said, I should have been paid the delay costs as well, just as I've been paid every other time in the past, because these delays were not my fault, and I did everything I was supposed to do. They're just trying to hide behind a technicality, now.

MR. BOCK: Counsel, I have no further questions, and we would also like a copy of the transcript.

MS. STEWART: Okay.

THE VIDEOGRAPHER: Okay. And this concludes—did you want me to conclude, counsel?

MS. STEWART: The deposition is concluded. Thank you.

THE VIDEOGRAPHER: Okay. This concludes today's deposition of Richard Brett. We are now going off record.

(The deposition was concluded.)

CERTIFICATE OF OATH

STATE OF NITA

I, the undersigned authority, certify that RICHARD BRETT personally appeared before me and was duly sworn on April 2, YR-1.

WITNESS my hand and official seal this 10th day of January, YR-0.

Daniel Perez

DANIEL PEREZ
Notary Commission Nita No. NN 389855
Commission Expires: November 28, YR+2

CERTIFICATE OF REPORTER

I, DANIEL PEREZ, a digital reporter and notary public within and for the State of Nita, do hereby certify:

That the foregoing witness whose examination is hereinbefore set forth was duly sworn and that said testimony was accurately captured with annotations by me during the proceeding.

I further certify that I am not related to any of the parties to this action by blood or marriage and that I have no interest in the outcome of this matter, financial or otherwise.

IN WITNESS THEREOF, I have hereunto set my hand this 10th day of January, YR-0.

Daniel Perez

DANIEL PEREZ
Notary Commission Nita No. NN 389855
Commission Expires: November 28, YR+2

CERTIFICATE OF TRANSCRIPTIONIST

I, Kalandra Lucas, legal transcriptionist, do hereby certify:

That the foregoing is a complete and true transcription of the original digital audio recording of the testimony and proceedings captured in the above-entitled matter. As the transcriptionist, I have reviewed and transcribed the entirety of the original digital audio recording of the proceeding to ensure a verbatim record to the best of my ability.

I further certify that I am neither attorney for nor a relative or employee of any of the parties to the action; further, that I am not a relative or employee of any attorney employed by the parties hereto, nor financially or otherwise interested in the outcome of this matter.

IN WITNESS THEREOF, I have hereunto set my hand this 10th day of January, YR-0.

Kalandra Lucas

Kalandra Lucas
Legal Transcriptionist

IN THE STATE OF NITA
NITA COUNTY CIRCUIT COURT

BRETT GENERAL CONTRACTING, LLC, a Nita corporation,

Plaintiff,

v.

THE SCHOOL BOARD OF NITA COUNTY,

Defendant.

CASE NO. 2-31869(12)(B)

VIDEO DEPOSITION OF

THOMAS A. SMITH

April 3, YR-1

9:30 a.m.

Remote Proceeding
Nita City, Nita

DANIEL PEREZ
Digital Reporter
Commission No. NN 389855

APPEARANCES OF COUNSEL

On behalf of Plaintiff, Brett General Contracting, LLC:

ERNIE BOCK, JR., ESQ.
BOCK, BOCK & ASSOCIATES
1251 Main Street
Suite 2500
Nita City, Nita 57818
APPEARED VIA VIDEOCONFERENCE

On behalf of Defendant, the School Board of Nita County:

MARSHA STEWART, ESQ.
STEWART LAW, P.A.
432 Hill Street
Nita City, Nita 57818
APPEARED VIA VIDEOCONFERENCE

Also Present:

Jordan McHugh, Videographer

INDEX TO EXAMINATION

INDEX OF EXHIBITS

(No exhibits marked.)

THE VIDEOGRAPHER: We are now on the record. The time is 9:30 a.m. on Sunday, April 3, YR-1. This begins the videotaped deposition of Thomas Smith taken in the matter of Brett General Contracting versus the School Board of Nita County, filed in the Circuit Court of the Tenth Judicial Circuit in and for Nita County, Nita; case number 2-31869(12)(B).

The videographer today is Jordan McHugh. The court reporter today is Daniel Perez. We are both representing eScribe Transcriptions.

Counsel, will you please announce your name and whom you represent, after which our court reporter will swear in the witness.

MR. BOCK: Ernie Bock, Jr. for Plaintiff, Brett General Contracting, LLC.

MS. STEWART: Marsha Stewart for Defendants, the School Board of Nita County.

THE REPORTER: Good morning, everyone. My name is Daniel Perez, notary public and digital reporter for eScribe Transcriptions in the state of Nita. I will be capturing the verbatim record of today's proceeding using electronic audio equipment, a computer, and specialized recording software, which is not a form of stenography.

The witness is presently located in Nita City,

Nita and has confirmed his identity by driver's license. Absent any objections at this time, counsel and the witness agree to my remote administration of the oath to the witness and that the final transcript may be used for all purposes allowed by local rules of civil procedure.

Hearing no objections, this shall constitute agreement and stipulation of such, and I will now swear in the witness.

Mr. Smith, please raise your right hand to be sworn.

THOMAS A. SMITH,

having first been duly sworn, testified as follows:

THE WITNESS: I do.

THE REPORTER: Okay. Counsel, you may begin.

EXAMINATION

BY MS. STEWART:

Q. Good morning, Mr. Smith. You're under—

A. Good morning.

Q. You understand that you are under oath and that being under oath means you are sworn to tell the truth?

A. Yes.

Q. Have you ever had your deposition taken in the past?

A. Yes, I have.
Q. And you understand that your responses here have the same force as in a courtroom with a judge and a jury?
A. Yes. Yes.
Q. Are you prepared to answer my questions today?
A. Yeah—yes. Of course.
Q. There isn't anything that will prevent you from providing me your full attention?
A. No.
Q. Have you taken any medication that can alter your ability to answer these questions?
A. No, I haven't taken anything.
Q. Will you let me know if you don't understand one of my questions so that I may repeat it clearly and make sure that you understand it clearly?
A. Yes.
Q. If you need to take a break at any time, just let me know. We'll take a break. Is that okay?
A. Yep. Yep.
Q. Okay. What is your full name, please?
A. Thomas A. Smith.
Q. Have you ever used any other names?
A. No.
Q. Do you have any nicknames?

A. People call me Tom.

Q. Do you have any licenses or certifications?

A. Yes. I have a project manager certification.

Q. Have you ever been arrested?

A. No.

Q. Have you ever been convicted of a crime?

A. No.

Q. Have you been involved in any other legal claims or lawsuit?

A. No.

Q. And how did you prepare for this deposition today?

A. I didn't—I didn't prepare.

Q. You didn't even meet with counsel for either party?

A. No.

Q. Mr. Smith, where are you employed?

A. I was employed by The School Board of Nita County, but I'm no longer working. I went on disability in YR-3.

Q. Okay. Let's discuss the project at hand in this lawsuit. Do you know which project we're here about today?

A. Yes. The project at 1532 Nita Road, Nita City, Nita 57818.

Q. And it is your job to work with the general contractor or it was your job to work with the general contractor in this case, Richard Brett, to get the project completed successfully on time; is that correct?

A. Yes. I supervised the project, and I'm the go between the general contractor and the school board.

Q. Are you aware that the contract between the general contractor, Richard Brett Contracting, and the school board have specific requirements for submitting any change orders to the project that would affect the cost or time for completion of the project?

A. I haven't seen the contract.

Q. How do you normal [sic] handle change orders that are submitted to you?

A. Pretty informal. As long as the GC sends me the request in some form of writing, I usually get it approved.

Q. And you submit it to the school board for approval?

A. Oh, yes. I have to.

Q. Interesting. All right. Let's walk through the payment process on this particular project. Work commenced on March 10, YR-3, when the contract was signed, and then Mr. Brett submitted an initial change

order with some minor modifications on April 22, YR-3. Is that correct?
A. Yes.
Q. Looking at this change order that we previously marked as Exhibit 3, is this the change order that you submitted to the school board on this project?
A. Let me review. Give me one second here.
Yes, I submitted this change order to the school board and they approved it. I believe it was paid.
Q. Are you aware of any other modifications to this project that affected the general contractor's cost or delays in meeting the project completion dates?
A. Yes. Mr. Brett asked for a shutdown exemption during the pandemic, which I didn't get to answer because I was sick. He left multiple voicemails, but I just couldn't respond. Then he sent me another change order due to my delay in getting back to him about the shutdown exemption and they—he had to pay for things like storage fees, payroll, and equipment rentals.
Q. Well, let's look at previously marked Composite Exhibit 4. Is this the email and change order that you are referring to?
A. Yes, it is.

Q. Do you recall whether you submitted this to the school board for payment and whether it was paid?

A. I didn't and it wasn't. I was very ill. I meant to, and I told Rich that I would, but I didn't.

Q. When did you tell Rich that?

A. I left him a voicemail.

MS. STEWART: Let's listen to this voicemail.

(Audio played.)

BY MS. STEWART:

Q. Is this the audio of the actual voicemail previously marked as Exhibit 5 that you left Mr. Brett on July 6, YR-3?

A. Yes. This is the voicemail that I left.

Q. What happened next?

A. I left. I went out on disability. Kelly [sic] Marks took over the project for me.

Q. Do you know what happened to this particular change order after that?

A. No. But I guess it didn't get paid because we're here doing this.

MS. STEWART: Counsel, I have no further questions, but we would like a copy of the transcript. Any questions on cross?

MR. BOCK: Yes, just a few.

//

EXAMINATION

BY MR. BOCK:

Q. Good morning, Mr. Smith.

A. Good morning.

Q. How many years did you work as a project manager for the school board?

A. About 17 years, give or take.

Q. Why are you testifying on behalf of the plaintiff today?

A. Well, it's because I had a health scare and I wasn't sure if I was going to make it. And I promised myself that if I came out okay, that I would do whatever it was I had to do to make the world right. And I believe this is the right thing to do.

MR. BOCK: Well, thank you, Mr.—Mr. Smith. We appreciate your time today. I have no further questions.

But we'll take a copy of the transcript as well.

MS. STEWART: Okay. We'll conclude this deposition.

Thank you, Mr. Smith, for appearing today.

THE WITNESS: You're welcome.

THE VIDEOGRAPHER: All righty.

THE WITNESS: You're welcome.

THE VIDEOGRAPHER: This concludes the deposition of Thomas Smith. We are now going off record.

(The deposition was concluded.)

CERTIFICATE OF OATH

STATE OF NITA

I, the undersigned authority, certify that THOMAS A. SMITH personally appeared before me and Was duly sworn on the 3rd day of April, YR-1.

WITNESS my hand and official seal this 10th day of January, YR-0.

Daniel Perez

DANIEL PEREZ
Notary Commission Nita No. NN 389855
Commission Expires: November 28, YR+2

CERTIFICATE OF REPORTER

I, DANIEL PEREZ, a digital reporter and notary public within and for the State of Nita do hereby certify:

That the foregoing witness whose examination is hereinbefore set forth was duly sworn and that said testimony was accurately captured with annotations by me during the proceeding.

I further certify that I am not related to any of the parties to this action by blood or marriage and that I have no interest in the outcome of this matter, financial or otherwise.

IN WITNESS THEREOF, I have hereunto set my hand this 10th day of January, YR-0.

Daniel Perez
DANIEL PEREZ
Notary Commission Nita No. NN 389855
Commission Expires: November 28, YR+2

CERTIFICATE OF TRANSCRIPTIONIST

I, Kalandra Lucas, legal transcriptionist, do hereby certify:

That the foregoing is a complete and true transcription of the original digital audio recording of the testimony and proceedings captured in the above-entitled matter. As the transcriptionist, I have reviewed and transcribed the entirety of the original digital audio recording of the proceeding to ensure a verbatim record to the best of my ability.

I further certify that I am neither attorney for nor a relative or employee of any of the parties to the action; further, that I am not a relative or employee of any attorney employed by the parties hereto, nor financially or otherwise interested in the outcome of this matter.

IN WITNESS THEREOF, I have hereunto set my hand this 10th day of January, YR-0.

Kalandra Lucas

Kalandra Lucas
Legal Transcriptionist

IN THE STATE OF NITA
NITA COUNTY CIRCUIT COURT

BRETT GENERAL CONTRACTING,)
LLC, a Nita corporation,)
0
Plaintiff,) CASE NO.
) 2-31869(12)(B)
)
v.)
)
THE SCHOOL BOARD)
OF NITA COUNTY,)
)
Defendant.)

VIDEO DEPOSITION OF CAROL MARKS

April 3, YR-1

11:30 a.m.

Remote Proceeding
Nita City, Nita

DANIEL PEREZ
Digital Reporter
Commission No. NN 389855

APPEARANCES OF COUNSEL

On behalf of Plaintiff, Brett General Contracting, LLC:

ERNIE BOCK, JR., ESQ.
BOCK, BOCK & ASSOCIATES
1251 Main Street
Suite 2500
Nita City, Nita 57818
APPEARED VIA VIDEOCONFERENCE

On behalf of Defendant, the School Board of Nita County:

MARSHA STEWART, ESQ.
STEWART LAW, P.A.
432 Hill Street
Nita City, Nita 57818
APPEARED VIA VIDEOCONFERENCE

Also Present:

Jordan McHugh, Videographer

INDEX TO EXAMINATION

INDEX OF EXHIBITS

(No exhibits marked.)

THE VIDEOGRAPHER: Good morning. We are now on the record. The time is 11:30 a.m. on Sunday, April 3, YR-1. This begins the videotaped deposition of Carol Marks, taken in the matter of Brett General Contracting versus the School Board of Nita County, filed in the Circuit Court of the 10th Judicial Circuit in and for Nita County, Nita; case number 2-31869(12)(B).

The videographer today is Jordan McHugh. The court reporter today is Daniel Perez. We are both representing eScribe Transcriptions.

Counsel, will you please announce your name and whom you represent, after which the court reporter will swear in our witness.

MR. BOCK: Ernie Bock, Jr., representing plaintiff.

Counsel, I think you're muted if you're trying to make your appearance.

MS. STEWART: Thank you. Nothing like having that on the record.

Marsha Stewart for defendant, School Board of Nita County.

THE REPORTER: Good morning, everyone. My name is Daniel Perez, notary public and digital reporter for eScribe Transcriptions in the state of Nita. I will be capturing the verbatim record of today's proceeding using electronic audio equipment, a computer, and specialized recording software, which is not a form of stenography. The witness is presently located in Nita City, Nita, and has confirmed her identity by driver's license.

Absent any objections at this time, counsel and the witness agree to my remote administration of the oath to the witness and that the final transcript may be used for all purposes allowed by local rules of civil procedure. Hearing no objections, this shall constitute agreement and stipulation of such and I will now swear in the witness.

Ms. Marks, please raise your right hand to be sworn.

CAROL M. MARKS,

having first been duly sworn, testified as follows:

THE WITNESS: I do.

THE REPORTER: Okay. Counsel, you may begin.

EXAMINATION

BY MR. BOCK:

Q. Good morning, Ms. Marks. You understand that by being placed under oath just now, you're sworn to tell the truth?

A. Yes, I understand that.

Q. Have you ever had your deposition taken in the past?
A. I have.
Q. Do you understand that your responses here have the same force as if made in a courtroom with a judge and a jury?
A. I understand that.
Q. Are you prepared to answer my questions today?
A. I am.
Q. There isn't anything that would prevent you from providing me your full attention today?
A. No.
Q. Have you taken any medication that can alter your ability to answer my questions?
A. No, I have not.
Q. And you'll let me know if you don't understand one of my questions. I have no problem repeating or rephrasing, but if you don't tell me you don't understand, I'll assume you understand the question.
A. That sounds fair.
Q. And if you need a break at any time, just tell me and we'll take a break. The only question or only thing I ask is, if there's a question pending, you just answer the pending question before we take the break. Is that okay?

A. That's okay with me. Thank you.

Q. And can you state your full name, please.

A. My full name is Carol M. Marks.

Q. Have you ever used any other names?

A. No.

Q. Do you have any nicknames?

A. No, I don't.

Q. You don't have any licenses or certifications?

A. I do. I have one. I am a certified project manager.

Q. Have you ever been arrested?

A. No.

Q. Have you ever been convicted of a crime?

A. No.

Q. Have you been involved in any other legal claims or lawsuits in the past?

A. No, I have not.

Q. And how did you prepare for this deposition?

A. Well, the only thing I actually did, I reviewed my notes that I had with respect to the project, but that was really about it.

Q. Did you meet with counsel?

A. I did not.

Q. Okay. And where are you currently employed?

A. I'm currently employed by the school board for

Nita City. I've been employed there for about 10 years.

Q. Okay. Let's discuss the project at hand. Do you know which project we're here about today?

A. Yes, I'm familiar with the project. It's the one at 1532 Nita Road, Nita City 57818.

Q. And is your job to work with the general contractor, which in this case was Richard Brett, to get the project completed successfully and on time?

A. Yes. That's—that's my role. I supervise the project and I'm sort of the go between the general contractor and the school board.

Q. Are you aware that the contract between the general contractor and the school board had specific requirements for submitting any changes to the project that would affect the cost or time for completion of the project?

A. Yes, I'm aware of that.

Q. How do you normally handle change orders that are submitted to you?

A. Well, once I receive them, I then submit them to the school board for approval.

Q. Okay. Let's walk through the payment process on this project. Work commenced on 10 March YR-3 when the contract was signed, and you came onto the project

3 August YR-3, and then Mr. Brett submitted a change order via email on 24 June YR-2; is that correct?

A. That's what I remember, yes.

Q. Well, let's look at this email to you, which was previously marked as Composite Exhibit 6. Is this the email you remember receiving on 24 June YR-2?

A. Yeah. That—that's the email I received.

Q. Are you aware whether Mr. Brett had previously submitted this change order?

A. I believe he did. I think he sent it to my predecessor, Tom Smith.

Q. Do you know why it was not paid and Mr. Brett was resubmitting it to you?

A. I think it was because Tom got sick and I think—and Richard never got paid.

Q. Do you recall what the delay was caused by?

A. Well, again, I think Tom was sick. He may have been ill, something. Oh, yeah. And the pandemic. Tom didn't get him an exemption to for outdoor work.

Q. So, nothing that was the fault of Mr. Brett?

A. Not to my knowledge.

Q. Okay. Did you submit the change order to the school board?

A. I did.

Q. What happened next?

A. Well, I was told they would approve it. You know, that's the policy. Like I had mentioned before, I—once I received them, I submit them to the school board for approval.

Q. You mentioned that they told you they would approve it. Who specifically told you that?

A. That I—I don't remember.

Q. Was it someone on the school board?

A. You know, to tell—you know, I—I don't I—I—honestly, I don't remember who it was. Probably someone on the school board.

Q. Okay. Well, once you learned that the school board would approve the change order, what did you do?

A. Actually, I went to tell Richard. And when I went in there, he wasn't in his office. It was—actually, I think he may have left early because it was his birthday. I think he had maybe (indiscernible) for birthday.

I remember I left him a note, and I recall thinking at the time, oh, that's actually a nice birthday present for him.

BY MR. BOCK:

Q. Is what I'm showing you now, the handwritten note, which was previously marked as Exhibit 7, that you left for Mr. Brett?

A. Yeah. That's the note.

Q. To your knowledge, did he ever get paid for that second change order?

A. No. Actually, the school board denied it.

Q. Do you know why the school board decided to deny payment for the second change order?

A. I really I—I don't remember.

Q. Okay. I'm showing you now a set of emails dated 22 April YR-2 and 23 June YR-2, previously marked as Composite Exhibit 9. Are these the emails you sent to Mr. Brett asking him about project completion status?

A. Yes. Those are the emails that I sent him because the project was delayed.

Q. Did he ultimately finish the project?

A. Yes, actually, he did finish, but it was about a month late. And I approved the completion after the inspection, as I was required to do according to the contract.

Q. Was he ever paid for that second change order?

A. No. That's why we're here.

Q. Do you know if Mr. Brett is still working on new projects with the school board?

A. Yes, I—I do know that. And yes, he is still working with the school board.

Q. Do you know why?

A. Actually, yeah, there's only a few companies that actually have been approved by the school board to do work for it. Approval is actually a really long and complicated process, and because of that, we don't have a lot of options to use. And so, if there's a company that's already been approved and they're not just absolutely terrible and they do, I guess, a good job, we'll hire them again. We don't have any issue with that.

MR. BOCK: Thank you, Ms. Marks.

Counsel, I have no further questions, but we would like a copy of the transcripts. Any questions on cross?

MS. STEWART: No questions for Ms. Marks.

MR. BOCK: We'll conclude this deposition. Thank you.

MS. STEWART: Thank you.

THE REPORTER: All right. This concludes today's deposition of Carol Marks. We're now going off record.

(The deposition was concluded.)

CERTIFICATE OF OATH

STATE OF NITA

I, the undersigned authority, certify that CAROL MARKS personally appeared before me and was duly sworn on April 3, YR-1.

WITNESS my hand and official seal this 10th day of January, YR-0.

Daniel Perez

DANIEL PEREZ
Notary Commission Nita No. NN 389855
Commission Expires: November 28, YR+2

CERTIFICATE OF REPORTER

I, DANIEL PEREZ, a digital reporter and notary public within and for the State of Nita do hereby certify:

That the foregoing witness whose examination is hereinbefore set forth was duly sworn and that said testimony was accurately captured with annotations by me during the proceeding.

I further certify that I am not related to any of the parties to this action by blood or marriage and that I have no interest in the outcome of this matter, financial or otherwise.

IN WITNESS THEREOF, I have hereunto set my hand this 10th day of January, YR-0.

Daniel Perez

DANIEL PEREZ
Notary Commission Nita No. NN 389855
Commission Expires: November 28, YR+2

CERTIFICATE OF TRANSCRIPTIONIST

I, Kalandra Lucas, legal transcriptionist, do hereby certify:

That the foregoing is a complete and true transcription of the original digital audio recording of the testimony and proceedings captured in the above-entitled matter. As the transcriptionist, I have reviewed and transcribed the entirety of the original digital audio recording of the proceeding to ensure a verbatim record to the best of my ability.

I further certify that I am neither attorney for nor a relative or employee of any of the parties to the action; further, that I am not a relative or employee of any attorney employed by the parties hereto, nor financially or otherwise interested in the outcome of this matter.

IN WITNESS THEREOF, I have hereunto set my hand this 10th day of January, YR-0.

Kalandra Lucas
Kalandra Lucas
Legal Transcriptionist

Deposition Testimony of Carol Marks
taken on April 3, YR-1

ERRATA SHEET

PAGE 9 **LINE** 3 **CHANGE** "That's what I remember, Yes." It should say "No, work commenced on April 1st, YR-3."

REASON The contract was signed on March 10th. Work actually commenced on April 1st.

PAGE_____ LINE_____ CHANGE________________________

____

REASON____

PAGE_____ LINE_____ CHANGE________________________

____

REASON____

PAGE_____ LINE_____ CHANGE________________________

____

REASON____

Under penalties of perjury, I declare that I have read the foregoing document and that the facts stated in it are true.

NAME	DATE
Carol Marks	4/5/YR-1

eScribe Transcriptions

819.555.DEPO(3376)
eScribeTranscriptions.nita

IN THE STATE OF NITA
NITA COUNTY CIRCUIT COURT

BRETT GENERAL CONTRACTING, LLC, a Nita corporation,

Plaintiff,

v.

THE SCHOOL BOARD OF NITA COUNTY,

Defendant.

CASE NO. 2-31869(12)(B)

VIDEO DEPOSITION OF

HOLLY PHYLLIS WILLIAMS

April 3, YR-1

1:30 p.m.

Remote Proceeding
Nita City, Nita

DANIEL PEREZ
Digital Reporter
Commission No. NN 389855

APPEARANCES OF COUNSEL

On behalf of Plaintiff, Brett General Contracting, LLC:

ERNIE BOCK, JR., ESQ.
BOCK, BOCK & ASSOCIATES
1251 Main Street
Suite 2500
Nita City, Nita 57818
APPEARED VIA VIDEOCONFERENCE

On behalf of Defendant, the School Board of Nita County:

MARSHA STEWART, ESQ.
STEWART LAW, P.A.
432 Hill Street
Nita City, Nita 57818
APPEARED VIA VIDEOCONFERENCE

Also Present:

Jordan McHugh, Videographer

INDEX TO EXAMINATION

INDEX OF EXHIBITS

(Exhibit 11 was attached to the original transcript.)

THE VIDEOGRAPHER: Good afternoon. We are now on the record. The time is 1:30 p.m. on Sunday, April 3, YR-1. This begins the videotaped deposition of Holly Williams, taken in the matter of Brett General Contracting versus the School Board of Nita County, filed in the Circuit Court of the Tenth Judicial Circuit in and for Nita County, Nita; case number 2-31869(12)(B).

The videographer today is Jordan McHugh. The court reporter today is Daniel Perez. We are both representing eScribe Transcriptions.

Counsel, will you please announce your name and whom you represent, after which our court reporter will swear in the witness.

MR. BOCK: Ernie Bock, Jr. for the plaintiff, Brett General Contracting, LLC.

MS. STEWART: Marsha Stewart for defendant, School Board of Nita County.

THE REPORTER: Good afternoon, everyone. My name is Daniel Perez, notary public and digital reporter for eScribe Transcriptions in the state of Nita. I will be capturing the verbatim record of today's proceeding using electronic audio equipment, a computer, and a specialized recording software, which is not a form of stenography. The witness is presently located in Nita City, Nita and has confirmed her identity by driver's license.

Absent any objections at this time, counsel and the witness agree to my remote administration of the oath to the witness and that the final transcript may be used for all purposes allowed by local rules of civil procedure.

Hearing no objections, this shall constitute agreement and stipulation of such and I will now swear in the witness.

Ms. Williams, please raise your right hand to be sworn.

HOLLY PHYLLIS WILLIAMS,

having first been duly sworn, testified as follows:

THE WITNESS: I do.

THE COURT: Okay. Counsel, you may begin.

EXAMINATION

BY MR. BOCK:

Q. Good morning, Ms. Williams. Thank you for being here today. I just want to confirm that you understand that you are under oath and that being under oath means you are sworn to tell the truth?

A. Yes.

Q. Have you ever had your deposition taken in the past?

A. Yes, I have.

Q. Good. Then you understand that your responses here have the same force as if they were made in a courtroom in front of a judge and jury?

A. Yes, I do.

Q. Are you prepared to answer my questions today?

A. Yes.

Q. And there isn't anything that will prevent you from providing me your full attention?

A. No.

Q. Have you taken any medications that can alter your ability to answer these questions?

A. I have not.

Q. If you don't understand one of my questions, please just tell me you don't understand. I'm more than happy to rephrase it. But if you don't tell me that you don't understand the question, I'm going to assume you do. Is that fair?

A. Yes, it is.

Q. And if you need to take a break at any time, just tell me and take a break. I only ask that if there's a question pending, you answer that question before we take a break. Is that also fair?

A. That's fair.

Q. And what is your full name?

A. Holly Phyllis Williams.

Q. Have you ever used any other names?

A. No.

Q. Do you have any nicknames?

A. No.

Q. Have you ever been arrested?

A. Of course not.

Q. Have you ever been convicted of any crimes?

A. Absolutely not.

Q. Have you been involved in any other legal claims or lawsuits?

A. No. None.

Q. How did you prepare for this deposition today?

A. I didn't prepare. There's nothing to prepare. I don't know why I'm even here.

Q. You didn't meet with counsel?

A. No.

Q. Are you a member of the School Board of Nita County?

A. Yes, I am.

Q. Okay. Let's discuss why we're here. Do you know which project this lawsuit is about?

A. Yes.

Q. And which project is that? What is the address of the school?

A. It's 1532 Nita Road, Nita City, Nita 57818.

Q. And as a school board member, is one of your duties to approve change orders submitted in regard to construction projects?

A. Yes, if it's on the agenda.

Q. Let's look at the first change order, which has previously been marked as Exhibit 3. Do you recall seeing and approving this change order?

A. No, but it would say it is in the minutes if I—if we did approve it.

Q. Okay. I'm going to show you the minutes dated May 3, YR-3, approving the first change order and the check made out to Mr. Brett's company. Does this help your recollection?

A. Yes.

Q. Wonderful.

MR. BOCK: Let's mark this as Exhibit 11 to the deposition. Thank you.

(Exhibit 11 was marked for identification.)

BY MR. BOCK:

Q. Exhibit 3, the first change order, is dated April 22, YR-3, correct?

A. I don't see where you—

Q. Middle of the page. Both Richard Brett and Sonia Forester signed and dated it 4/22/YR-3.

A. Okay, I see that now. Yes.
Q. And Exhibit 11,the school board minutes approving the first change order and the check paying the first change order. Do you have those?
A. Yes.
Q. What is the date of the school board meeting?
A. May 3, YR-3.
Q. And on what date was the check for the first change order issued?
A. Oh. May 2. But that could be because they were running checks—
Q. Thank you.
A. It might not have been mailed—
Q. Please just answer my questions. Did the school board meet and approve the first change order prior to Sonia Forester signing off as the project manager?
A. No.
Q. Did the school board meet and approve the first change order before the check for it was written?
A. No.
Q. Now, please take a look at this email dated 3 September YR-3, with its attached change order, which has previously been marked as Composite Exhibit 6. Do you recall seeing this ever?
A. I don't recall if I did. It would be in the

minutes of the meeting—it would be in the meeting of the minutes, and it would have been approved or denied.

Q. Okay. Let me show you a letter dated 22 February YR-2 from you to the plaintiff, Mr. Brett. It's previously been marked as Exhibit 8.

Let me know if this helps your recollection.

A. Yes. Looks like we denied the change order because he didn't submit it to the school board for approval.

Q. Are you aware that both project managers on this project, Tom Smith and Carol Marks, told Mr. Brett that the change order would be approved and that he would be paid?

A. Yes. But they don't have the authority, so we are not bound by anything they say.

Q. Please take a look at what's previously been marked as Exhibit 7. This is a Post-it note which was left for Mr. Brett by Ms. Marks indicating that the second change order would be paid.

Have you ever seen this note before?

A. No, I have not.

Q. Your letter references a no-damages-for-delay clause in the contract?

A. Yes. It's in all of our contracts.

Q. Are you aware that Mr. Brett had been paid for delays on previous projects with the school board?

A. I'm not aware, but I'm also not surprised. You must know that a grand jury decided that the school board paid too much money to contract—to contractors, and that's the audit—and that the audit determined we should not be paying delay damages due to the clause in the contracts. We had not been following the clause in the past, and then we got strict about it.

Q. Moving back onto the subject of the project this lawsuit's about, do you know if this project was finished?

A. I believe it was.

Q. Do you know whether Mr. Brett was ever paid for the delay damages?

A. No, he was not.

Q. Do you know whether Mr. Brett is still working on new projects with the school board?

A. Yes. We do continue to hire his company.

MR. BOCK: Thank you for being here, Ms. Williams. I have nothing further for you. We'll order a copy of the transcript. Counsel, do you have any questions for cross.

MS. STEWART: No cross at this time of Ms. Williams.

And we would also like a copy of the transcript, please.

MR. BOCK: All right. That will conclude this deposition.

THE VIDEOGRAPHER: Okay. We'll quick, counsel, before I take us off record. Will, either of you be ordering a video today?

MS. STEWART: Defense counsel would like a copy of the video and have it synced, please.

THE VIDEOGRAPHER: Perfect.

All right. Mr. Bock?

MR. BOCK: We'll take the video as well. Synced, expedited.

THE VIDEOGRAPHER: Perfect. All right. Then this concludes today's deposition of Holly Williams. We are now going off record.

(The deposition was concluded.)

CERTIFICATE OF OATH

STATE OF NITA

I, the undersigned authority, certify that HOLLY PHYLLIS WILLIAMS personally appeared before me and was duly sworn on the 3rd day of April, YR-1.

WITNESS my hand and official seal this 10th day of January, YR-0.

Daniel Perez

DANIEL PEREZ
Notary Commission Nita No. NN 389855
Commission Expires: November 28, YR+2

HOLLY PHYLLIS WILLIAMS April 03, YR-1
BRETT GENERAL vs SBNC 14

CERTIFICATE OF REPORTER

I, DANIEL PEREZ, a digital reporter and notary public within and for the State of Nita do hereby certify:

That the foregoing witness whose examination is hereinbefore set forth was duly sworn and that said testimony was accurately captured with annotations by me during the proceeding.

I further certify that I am not related to any of the parties to this action by blood or marriage and that I have no interest in the outcome of this matter, financial or otherwise.

IN WITNESS THEREOF, I have hereunto set my hand this 10th day of January, YR-0.

Daniel Perez
DANIEL PEREZ
Notary Commission Nita No. NN 389855
Commission Expires: November 28, YR+2

eScribe Transcriptions 819.555.DEPO(3376)
eScribeTranscriptions.nita

CERTIFICATE OF TRANSCRIPTIONIST

I, Kalandra Lucas, legal transcriptionist, do hereby certify:

That the foregoing is a complete and true transcription of the original digital audio recording of the testimony and proceedings captured in the above-entitled matter. As the transcriptionist, I have reviewed and transcribed the entirety of the original digital audio recording of the proceeding to ensure a verbatim record to the best of my ability.

I further certify that I am neither attorney for nor a relative or employee of any of the parties to the action; further, that I am not a relative or employee of any attorney employed by the parties hereto, nor financially or otherwise interested in the outcome of this matter.

IN WITNESS THEREOF, I have hereunto set my hand this 10th day of January, YR-0.

Kalandra Lucas
Kalandra Lucas
Legal Transcriptionist

IN THE STATE OF NITA
NITA COUNTY CIRCUIT COURT

BRETT GENERAL CONTRACTING, LLC, a Nita corporation,	)) 0	
Plaintiff,	)))	CASE NO. 2-31869(12)(B)
v.	))	
THE SCHOOL BOARD IF NITA COUNTY,	)))	
Defendant.	)	

VIDEO DEPOSITION OF ERIC MAYPER

April 2, YR-1

11:30 a.m.

Remote Proceeding
Nita City, Nita

DANIEL PEREZ
Digital Reporter
Commission No. NN 389855

APPEARANCES OF COUNSEL

On behalf of Plaintiff, Brett General Contracting, LLC:

ERNIE BOCK, JR., ESQ.
BOCK, BOCK & ASSOCIATES
1251 Main Street
Suite 2500
Nita City, Nita 57818
APPEARED VIA VIDEOCONFERENCE

On behalf of Defendant, the School Board of Nita County:

MARSHA STEWART, ESQ.
STEWART LAW, P.A.
432 Hill Street
Nita City, Nita 57818
APPEARED VIA VIDEOCONFERENCE

Also Present:

Jordan McHugh, Videographer

INDEX TO EXAMINATION

INDEX OF EXHIBITS

(No exhibits marked.)

THE VIDEOGRAPHER: Good morning. We are now on the record. The time is 11:30 a.m. on Saturday, April 2, YR-1. This begins the videotaped deposition of Eric Mayper, taken in the matter of Brett General Contracting versus the School Board of Nita County, filed in the Circuit Court of the 10th Judicial Circuit in and for Nita County, Nita; case number 2-31869(12)(B).

The videographer today is Jordan McHugh. The court reporter today is Daniel Perez. We are both representing eScribe Transcriptions.

Counsel, will you please announce your name and whom you represent, after which the court reporter will swear in our witness.

MR. BOCK: Ernie Bock, Jr., representing plaintiff.

MS. STEWART: Marsha Stewart for defendants, School Board of Nita County.

THE REPORTER: Good morning, everyone. My name is Daniel Perez, notary public and digital reporter for eScribe Transcriptions in the state of Nita. I will be capturing the verbatim record today of today's proceeding using electronic audio equipment, a computer, and specialized recording software, which is not a form of stenography.

The witness is presently located in Nita City, Nita, and has confirmed his identity by driver's license. Absent any objections at this time, counsel and the witness agreed on my remote administration of the oath to the witness and that the final transcript may be used for all purposes allowed by local rules of civil procedure.

Hearing no objection, this shall constitute agreement and stipulation of such and I will now swear in the witness.

Mr. Mayper, please raise your right hand to be sworn.

ERIC MAYPER,

having first been duly sworn, testified as follows:

THE WITNESS: I do.

THE REPORTER: Okay. Counsel, you may begin.

EXAMINATION

BY MR. BOCK:

Q. Thank you for being here, Mr. Mayper. We appreciate you taking the time today to speak with us.

A. It's my pleasure. It's no trouble at all.

Q. Great. Let's begin with some housekeeping. You understand that you are under oath and that being under oath means you are sworn to tell the truth?

A. Yes.

Q. Have you ever had your deposition taken in the past as an expert?
A. Yes.
Q. For defendant's counsel?
A. No.
Q. For similar types of construction-related cases as an expert?
A. Yes.
Q. Have you ever testified as an expert against the School Board of Nita County?
A. It was one time, yes.
Q. Okay. What is your full name?
A. My name is Eric Mayper.
Q. Did you attend college?
A. Yes. I graduated from Nita College.
Q. Do you have any licenses or certifications?
A. Yes. I have a GC license.
Q. How long have you been working as a general contractor?
A. About 24 years. I owned my own construction business for 17 years. Now I'm semi-retired.
Q. And you are here today on behalf of the defendant, School Board of Nita County, correct?
A. Yes.
Q. Okay. How much do you charge for your time?

A. I charge $350 per hour.

Q. Okay. How did you prepare for your deposition today?

A. So, I reviewed the pleadings, the plans, the change orders that were submitted, and the contract.

Q. How many hours did that take you?

A. It took about five hours.

Q. Let's talk about the case now. You said that you were able to review the contract, correct?

A. Yes.

Q. Can you please describe the relevant portions of the contract related to this matter?

A. Sure. There are essentially the two clauses that stand out. The no-damages-for-delay clause, which is exactly what it sounds like, and the procedure for change orders to be submitted and approved.

Q. Let's discuss the no-damages-for-delay clause first. Can you explain what that clause means, please?

A. Of course, Clause 4.05 of the contract is a no damages for delay clause, which basically says that the contractor is not entitled to any extra compensation or time extension due to delay, with the exception of being an Act of God or active interference by the school board. And in that case, the remedy would only be an extension of time.

It even specifically mentions things like equipment, overhead, wages. It states that no moneys will be paid to those things above the contracted price.

Q. When you use the term "Act of God," what is an Act of God?

A. Like a hurricane, for example.

Q. Is a pandemic an Act of God in your expertise?

A. I don't think so. Most of the work, especially in the beginning of the contract, was outdoors. And even if it was indoors, there was plenty of ventilation.

Q. Do you know if some no-damages-for-delay clauses are now including pandemics as an Act of God?

A. Some are. I guess it depends on the parties and how they negotiate.

Q. Okay. That's fair. Have you ever done any work for the School Board of Nita County as a general contractor?

A. Yeah. It was once upon a very long time ago. Probably about 14 or 15 years ago.

Q. Do you recall a no-damages-for-delay clause in that contract?

A. Yes. And that's why I wouldn't do any other jobs for them. All construction projects experience delays because there are so many moving parts. It's impossible to predict everything.

Q. Okay. So, as a sophisticated businessman, you knew not to accept a contract with a clause like that in it?

A. Yes.

Q. Tell us about the other clauses you mentioned, the procedure for change orders specifically.

A. Well, the contract says also in 4.05 that extensions of time will only be permitted by change order.

Q. Well, let's back up a little bit. What is a change order exactly?

A. If something comes up that will change the project in some way, which can be the cost, like if we need to buy more materials or a delay, like there was a hurricane and everything had to be put into storage to protect it, then the contractor is obligated to submit the invoices, that's the change order, and get reimbursed if it's approved by the other party of the contract.

Q. When you work for the school board, did you submit any change orders?

A. Yes.
Q. For time or money?
A. Both.
Q. Was it approved?
A. For time, yes. For money, no.
Q. And were there change orders in this case?
A. Yes, for both time and money.
Q. Were they approved?
A. The first change order was approved, but the second one was not.
Q. Why not?
A. It was because it was never brought up on the agenda for the school board to assess and decide upon.
Q. And according to the contract, it must be brought up to the school board?
A. Yeah. On page 6 of 7 of the general conditions of the contract, it states that the change orders must be approved and signed by the owner, which is the school board. In order to do that, it must get on the agenda for the meeting. And according—and according to the minutes, it never was.
Q. So, the project manager or superintendent is not allowed to approve the change order?
A. The project manager, no. The superintendent, yes. But only up to 5 percent of the contract

price. Since this change order was more than the 5 percent, the school board has to approve it.

Q. What happens if the change order is not signed and approved?

A. The contractor has to continue with the work.

Q. And did Mr. Brett continue with and finish the work?

A. Yeah. And almost on time, too. Less than a month after the deadline, but still before the start of the school year.

Q. In this particular case, we have both a voicemail from the first project manager and a Post-it note from the second project manager assuring Mr. Brett that the second change order will be paid. Does that alter your opinion at all?

A. No. It doesn't matter what they say. The school board didn't approve it. He should have known that. I'm not sure why he continued to work on the projects for them.

Q. Mr. Brett says that he has signed the same contract in the past, and the change orders have always been paid, so he was not concerned. Why do you think previous change orders were paid on other projects?

A. Either got [sic] lucky or it's because of the

whole thing that happened a couple of years back with the grand jury. You know, they stopped paying, which, again, he should have known.

MR. BOCK: Thank you, Mr. Mayper.

Counsel, I have no further questions, but we would like a copy of the transcript. Any questions on cross?

MS. STEWART: None for this witness. And we, too, would like a copy of the transcript.

THE VIDEOGRAPHER: Okay. I'll go ahead and conclude. This concludes today's deposition of Eric Mayper. We're now going off record.

(The deposition was concluded.)

CERTIFICATE OF OATH

STATE OF NITA

I, the undersigned authority, certify that ERIC MAYPER personally appeared before me and was duly sworn on April 2, YR-1.

WITNESS my hand and official seal this 10th day of January, YR-0.

Daniel Perez

DANIEL PEREZ
Notary Commission Nita No. NN 389855
Commission Expires: November 28, YR+2

CERTIFICATE OF REPORTER

I, DANIEL PEREZ, a digital reporter and notary public within and for the State of Nita do hereby certify:

That the foregoing witness whose examination is hereinbefore set forth was duly sworn and that said testimony was accurately captured with annotations by me during the proceeding.

I further certify that I am not related to any of the parties to this action by blood or marriage and that I have no interest in the outcome of this matter, financial or otherwise.

IN WITNESS THEREOF, I have hereunto set my hand this 10th day of January, YR-0.

Daniel Perez
DANIEL PEREZ
Notary Commission Nita No. NN 389855
Commission Expires: November 28, YR+2

CERTIFICATE OF TRANSCRIPTIONIST

I, Kalandra Lucas, legal transcriptionist, do hereby certify:

That the foregoing is a complete and true transcription of the original digital audio recording of the testimony and proceedings captured in the above-entitled matter. As the transcriptionist, I have reviewed and transcribed the entirety of the original digital audio recording of the proceeding to ensure a verbatim record to the best of my ability.

I further certify that I am neither attorney for nor a relative or employee of any of the parties to the action; further, that I am not a relative or employee of any attorney employed by the parties hereto, nor financially or otherwise interested in the outcome of this matter.

IN WITNESS THEREOF, I have hereunto set my hand this 10th day of January, YR-0.

Kalandra Lucas

Kalandra Lucas
Legal Transcriptionist

Marked Exhibits

Exhibit 1

Construction Contract

THIS AGREEMENT made and entered into this 10th day of March, YR-3, by and between

THE SCHOOL BOARD OF NITA COUNTY

(hereinafter referred to as the **owner**) and

BRETT GENERAL CONTRACTING, LLC

(hereinafter referred to as the **contractor**).

WHEREAS, the owner owns certain real property located in Nita County (the **property**) which is currently improved, including the buildings known as Alan B. Whitfield Elementary School,

WHEREAS, the owner desires to have the following additional improvements made at the property: a) a cafeteria and b) eight classrooms (collectively the **project**),

WHEREAS, the project shall be constructed pursuant to drawings, specifications, and other design documents (collectively referred to as **project drawings**) prepared by

We Build Nita, Inc., Architects

(hereinafter referred to as the **project consultant**),

WHEREAS, the contractor agrees to provide all labor, services, and materials necessary to construct the project (hereinafter the **work**) in accordance with the project drawings and this contract (collectively, the **contract documents**) and all applicable laws, codes, and ordinances,

NOW THEREFORE, in exchange for the mutual covenants and promises set forth in this contract and the money the owner agrees to pay to the contractor, the parties agree as follows:

ARTICLE 1. ENTIRE AGREEMENT.

- 1.01 This construction contract embodies the entire agreement between owner and contractor and supersedes all other writings, oral agreements, or representations.
- 1.02 The parties shall not be bound by or be liable for any statement, representation, promise, inducement, or understanding of any kind or nature not set forth herein.
- 1.03 NO CHANGES, AMENDMENTS, OR MODIFICATIONS OF ANY OF THE TERMS OR CONDITIONS OF THE CONTRACT SHALL BE VALID UNLESS REDUCED TO WRITING AND SIGNED BY BOTH PARTIES.

CONTRACT SUM.

- 1.04 The owner shall pay, and the contractor shall accept, as full and complete payment for the contractor's timely performance of the work and contractor's other obligations, the fixed price of:

  Five million two hundred eighteen thousand dollars ($5,218,000)
  (the **contract sum**)

- which shall constitute the entire consideration to be paid to the contractor. The contract sum shall not be modified except by change order or by unit prices, if any, as provided in the contract documents.

ARTICLE 2. TIME FOR CONTRACTOR'S PERFORMANCE.

- 2.01 The contractor shall begin the work on 04/01/YR-3 (the **commencement date**) and shall diligently continue its performance until final completion of the project.
- 2.02 Deadline for Substantial Completion:
- 2.02.01 The contractor shall substantially complete the work on or before:

  June 20, YR-2

- 2.03 Liquidated Damages:
- 2.03.01 The contractor shall pay the owner five hundred dollars ($500.00) per day for each and every calendar day of unexcused delay in achieving substantial completion beyond 07/21/YR-2.
- 2.03.02 The owner and the contractor acknowledge that any sums due and payable by the contractor under this section 2.03 shall be payable, not as a penalty, but as liquidated damages representing a reasonable estimate of delay damages, inconvenience, additional overhead, and costs likely to be sustained by the owner, estimated at the time of executing this contract. If the owner reasonably believes in its discretion that substantial completion will be delayed, the owner shall be entitled, but not required, to withhold from any amounts otherwise due the contractor an amount then believed by the owner to be adequate to recover liquidated damages applicable to such delays. If and when in its discretion the contractor overcomes the delay in achieving substantial completion, or any part thereof, for which the owner has withheld payment, the owner shall promptly release to the contractor those funds withheld, as liquidated damages.
- 2.03.03 Partial use or occupancy of the work shall not result in the work being deemed substantially completed, and such partial use or occupancy shall not be evidence of substantial completion.

ARTICLE 3. SUBSTANTIAL COMPLETION AND FINAL PAYMENT.

- 3.01 Substantial Completion:
- 3.01.01 When the contractor believes that substantial completion has been achieved, the contractor shall notify the project consultant in writing and shall provide to the project consultant a listing of those matters, if any, yet to be finished. The project consultant will determine whether the work (or portion thereof) is appropriately ready for a substantial completion inspection.
- 3.01.02 If the project consultant determines the work is ready for a substantial completion inspection, the project consultant and owner will inspect the work to determine if the work is, in fact, substantially complete. If the project consultant and owner determine the work is not substantially complete, the project consultant shall advise the contractor in writing. If the project consultant and owner determine the work is substantially complete, the project consultant and owner shall prepare a list (the **punch list**) of items necessary for the contractor to correct, complete, or finish to reach final completion. When substantial completion is achieved, the project consultant will issue a letter formally establishing the substantial completion date for the work or portion thereof.
- 3.01.03 Upon substantial completion, the owner shall pay the contractor an amount sufficient to increase total payments to the contractor to the contract price, less a) any amounts attributable to liquidated damages, and b) 200 percent of the reasonable costs (as determined by the owner at its sole discretion), for i) completing all punch list items, ii) correcting and bringing into conformance all defective and nonconforming work, and iii) resolving any outstanding or threatened claims or any other matters that could cause the owner damage, cost, expense, or delay.
- 3.02 Final Completion:
- 3.02.01 When the contractor believes that the work, or portion thereof, is finally complete and is ready for a final inspection, the contractor shall notify the project consultant in writing. The project consultant will then determine whether the work (or portion thereof) is appropriately ready for a final completion inspection.
- 3.02.02 If the work is determined to be ready for a final completion inspection, the project consultant and owner will inspect the work to determine if the work is, in fact, finally complete. When the final completion inspection determines that the work is complete, the project consultant will issue a letter formally establishing the final completion date for the work or portion thereof.
- 3.02.03 When the project consultant and owner confirm that the project a) is complete in full accordance with the contract documents, b) has passed all required inspections,

including but not limited to those required by the State Department of Education, and/or from any and all governmental bodies, boards, entities, etc., and c) that the contractor has performed all of its obligations to the owner, the project consultant will approve final payment to the owner certifying to the owner that the project is complete and the contractor is entitled to the remainder of the unpaid contract price, less any amount withheld pursuant to contract documents.

- 3.03 Prior to being entitled to receive final payment, and as a condition precedent thereto, the contractor shall provide the owner, in the form and manner required by owner, if any, with a copy to the project consultant, of the following:
- 3.03.01 An affidavit that all of the contractor's obligations to subcontractors, laborers, equipment suppliers, or other third parties in connection with the project, have been paid or otherwise satisfied;
- 3.03.02 Such other documents that the owner requires from each subcontractor, lower tier subcontractor, laborer, supplier, or other person or entity who has or might have a claim against the owner, including but not limited to a right to assert a lien against the property;
- 3.03.03 All product warranties, operating manuals, instruction manuals, and other things or documents customarily required of the contractor, or reasonably required by the owner, including but not limited to those required elsewhere in the contract documents, as part of its project closeout procedures;
- 3.03.04 The owner shall, subject to its rights set forth in the contract documents, make final payment of all sums due to the contractor within thirty (30) days of the approval for final payment.

ARTICLE 4. TIME AND DELAYS.

- 4.01 All time in the contract documents is calculated on a consecutive calendar day basis.
- 4.02 Time is of the essence in this contract, and any breach of same shall go to the essence hereof. The contractor, in agreeing to complete the work within the time herein mentioned, has taken into consideration and made allowances for all reasonable hindrances and delays incident to its work.
- 4.03 The contractor agrees to begin work by the commencement date and to diligently and continuously perform the work and to coordinate the work with other work being performed on the project by other trades so that the owner shall not be delayed by any act or omission of contractor in completion of the project within the time specified above.
- 4.04 The contractor shall promptly pay its vendors, subcontractors, and suppliers and for labor, material, and equipment used by it in the performance of its work.

- 4.05 The contractor shall not be entitled to any claim for damages time on account of hindrance or delays from any cause whatsoever. However, if a delay is caused by any Act of God or active interference on the part of the owner, such act, hindrance, or delay may only entitle the contractor to receive an extension of time as its sole and exclusive remedy.
- 4.05.01 Adverse weather such as rain is not to be considered to be an Act of God unless it exceeds the ten-year average as published by the National Weather Service (or equivalent organization acceptable to the owner at its sole discretion) for that time of year in Nita County.
- 4.05.02 An extension of time to complete the work shall be determined by the owner provided that the contractor provides the owner with notice in writing of the cause of said act, hindrance, or delay within twenty (20) days after its occurrence.
- 4.05.03 In the event the request for extension is not made in writing within that twenty (20) day period, the contractor acknowledges and agrees it has forever waived any and all rights to such an extension.
- 4.05.04 All extensions of time shall be authorized only by a written change order executed by the owner and project consultant.
- 4.05.05 This "no damage for delay" clause encompasses any damages for delay or disruption even if the contractor completes construction of the work in a timely fashion in accordance with this contract.
- 4.05.06 Damages as referenced in this no damage for delay clause shall include any type of damages that are or could be awarded by any court or arbitration panel such as, by way of general example but not limited to, tort, contract, strict liability, consequential damages, liquidated damages, and/or punitive damages.
- 4.05.07 By way of specific example but not limitation, damages as referenced within this clause include loss of use, loss of profits, labor inefficiency, loss of bonding capacity, overhead and repair costs, costs of capital replacement, loss of wages, pain and suffering, loss of production costs to replace facilities, equipment and/or product loss, increased and/or extended home office overhead, increased general conditions, costs of mobilization and demobilization, decrease in value, and/or any other damage or loss.
- 4.05.08 The contractor recognizes and specifically acknowledges the terms and conditions of the no damage for delay clause upon execution of this contract.

ARTICLE 5. NOTICES

- 5.01 Any notices provided for hereunder shall be in writing and may be served either personally on the authorized representative of the receiving party at the jobsite, with a copy via telecopier or facsimile to the addresses shown below, or by registered mail or overnight delivery/courier service (e.g., Federal Express) to that party at the addresses shown below:

Party:		Address:
Owner Representative:	Marsha Stewart, Esquire Counsel for: School Board of Nita County, Nita	STEWART LAW, PA 432 Hill Street Nita City, NI 57818
Contractor:	Brett General Contracting, LLC	2301 NW 33rd Court, #102 Nita City, NI 57822
Project Consultant:	We Build Nita, Inc., Architects	1300 N. Main Avenue Nita, NI 57815

- 5.02 These notice addresses may be changed by written notice to the other addresses.

In Witness Whereof, the contractor, Brett General Contracting, LLC, and the owner, the School Board of Nita County, Nita, have signed and executed this contract by and through their duly authorized officers, on March 10, YR-3.

OWNER

THE SCHOOL BOARD OF NITA COUNTY, NITA

By: Robert Franklin, Jr.
Robert Franklin Jr.
Superintendent of Schools

CONTRACTOR

BRETT GENERAL CONTRACTING, LLC

By: Richard Brett
Richard Brett, President

Attest Secretary

William Brett, Sr.
William Brett, Sr.
Vice President/ Attest Secretary

DOCUMENT 00700

GENERAL CONDITIONS OF THE CONTRACT

THE WORK.

The contractor shall perform all of the work required by the contract documents and shall provide materials, supplies, tools, equipment, labor, and services directly related to the work, and shall perform the work in a good and workmanlike manner with sufficient manpower to perform the work in accordance with the time requirements set forth in the contract documents, and shall perform all other acts and supply all other things necessary to complete the work in strict accordance with the contract documents.

When completed, the work shall conform to the requirements of the contract documents and be completely ready for occupancy and finally completed.

The contractor represents and warrants to the owner the following:

It is financially solvent and has sufficient working capital to perform the obligations under this construction contract.

It is experienced and skilled in constructing the type of project described in the contract document.

It is able to provide the labor, materials, equipment, and machinery necessary to complete the work for the agreed upon price.

It is fully licensed under all applicable laws and authorized to do business in the State of Nita in the name of the entity identified as the contractor in the construction contract.

It has visited the jobsite and examined its nature and location, including without limitation: the surface conditions of the site and any structure or obstruction both natural or man-made; the surface water conditions and water ways of the site and surrounding area; the subsurface conditions of the land as disclosed by soil test borings; and the location of electric and utility lines and water, sanitary, sewer, and storm drain lines. The contractor acknowledges receipt and has reviewed the site geotechnical report as provided by the owner.

It will comply with all federal, state, and local governmental laws, rules, and regulations relating to its responsibilities as set forth in the contract documents.

COORDINATION AND CORRELATION OF DRAWINGS AND SPECIFICATIONS.

The contractor represents the following:

The contractor and subcontractors have fully examined and compared all drawings, specifications, and other contract documents, including but not limited to those relating to the architectural, structural, mechanical, electrical, civil engineering, and plumbing elements, and have compared and reviewed all general and specific details on the drawings and the various technical and administrative requirements of the specifications.

With respect to all construction materials, labor, methods, means, techniques, and sequence of procedures required to carry out the work or safety precautions and programs required in connection with carrying out the work, all conflicts, discrepancies, errors, and omissions that the contractor is aware of as a result of the examination and comparison of the contract documents have been either corrected or clarified to the satisfaction of the contractor prior to execution of this construction contract.

The contract sum is reasonable compensation and represents the total lump sum cost for the work and all systems and work shall be functional and in accordance with the requirements of the contract documents.

The contract time is adequate for the performance of the work.

The contractor is responsible for all means, methods, techniques, and sequencing of construction.

If, after execution of this construction contract, the contractor detects a conflict, discrepancy, error, or omission in the contract documents then it shall immediately notify the project consultant and the owner prior to proceeding with the specific portion of the work.

INTENT AND INTERPRETATION.

With respect to the intent and interpretation of this contract, the owner and the contractor agree as follows:

The contractor shall have a continuing duty to read, examine, review, compare, and contrast each of the documents which make up this contract and shall immediately give written notice to the owner and the project consultant of any conflict, ambiguity, error, or omission which the contractor may find with respect to these documents before proceeding with the affected work.

The intent of the contract documents is to include all labor and materials, equipment, and transportation necessary for the proper execution of the work. The contractor shall continually refer to drawings, specifications, and other contract documents in this regard.

In the event of a conflict among the contract documents, the most stringent requirement to the contractor shall control.

PROGRESS.

The contractor shall provide the owner with full information in advance as to its plans for performing each part of the work. This shall include, but not be limited to, schedules provided to the owner as post-award information and subsequently updated schedules submitted to the owner on a monthly basis as required elsewhere in the contract documents.

The contractor's schedule shall be updated no less frequently than monthly (unless the parties otherwise agree in writing) and shall be updated to reflect conditions encountered from time to time and shall apply to the total project.

Each such revision shall be provided to the owner and the project consultant.

Compliance with the requirements of this subparagraph shall be a condition precedent to payment to the contractor, and failure by the contractor to comply with these requirements shall constitute a material breach of this contract.

In receiving these schedules, the owner in no way acknowledges or consents that the schedules are acceptable or reasonable, but is simply reviewing same for its own informational purposes.

If at any time during the progress of work, the contractor's actual progress fails to meet the contract requirements, such as the required completion dates, the owner may notify the contractor, who shall take whatever steps necessary to improve its progress so as to complete the work on or before the required substantial completion date.

If within a reasonable period determined by the owner, the contractor does not improve performance to meet the contract requirements, such as the required completion dates, then the owner may require an increase in any or all of the following: contractor's subcontractor crews and contractor's own labor force, the number of shifts, overtime operation, contractor's supervision, and additional days of work per week, all without cost to owner.

Neither such notice by the owner nor the owner's failure to issue such notice shall relieve the contractor of its obligation to achieve the quality of work and rate of progress required by the contract.

Failure of the contractor to comply with the owner's instructions may be grounds for the owner to determine that the contractor is not prosecuting its work with the diligence that will assure completion within the time specified.

Upon such determination, the owner, in addition to any and all other rights set forth in the contract documents and remedies afforded owner under the contract documents or at law, may:

Elect to proceed with the work with its own employees, agents, contractors, subcontractors, and suppliers and assess all costs, expenses, or fees for same against the contractor and/or terminate for cause the contractor's right to proceed with the contracted work, or any separable part thereof, in accordance with the applicable provisions of the contract.

CONTRACT PAYMENTS.

The owner shall pay the contract price to the contractor in accordance with these procedures:

On or before the 15th day of each month after commencement of performance, but no more frequently than once monthly, the contractor may apply for payment for the period ending the last day of the previous month or other pay period the contractor and owner mutually define and agree to.

The contractor shall apply for payment in the format required elsewhere in the contract documents and include whatever supporting information required by the project consultant, the owner, or both. The contractor may request payment for 90 percent [the remaining 10 percent being the retainage] of that part of the contract sum allocable to the properly fulfilled contract requirements and the labor, material, and equipment properly incorporated in the project.

The contractor shall sign each payment application, which shall constitute the contractor's representation that the quantity of work has reached the level for which payment is requested, that the work has been properly installed or performed in substantial compliance with the requirements of the contract documents, and that the contractor knows of no reason why payment should not be made as requested.

The owner shall pay the contractor within thirty (30) days following the project consultant's written approval of each payment application.

Each payment shall be for the amount approved by the project consultant, less any amounts owing by the contractor to the owner or that the owner has the right to withhold as authorized by the contract documents or reasonable business practices.

The project consultant's approval of the contractor's applications for payment shall not preclude the owner from exercising any of its rights as set forth in the contract documents.

The contractor's application for payment also constitutes an affirmative representation and warranty that all work for which the owner has previously paid is free and clear of any lien, claim, or other encumbrance by any person whatsoever.

Prior to payment, the contractor shall, as required by the contract and as required by the owner, also provide the owner with documents relating to the project, including, but not limited to, updated schedules and daily logs and properly executed documents from all subcontractors, materialmen, suppliers, or others having rights acknowledging proper payment and waiving and relinquishing any rights or other claims relating to the project site.

Furthermore, the contractor warrants and represents that, upon payment of an application for payment, title to all work included in that application shall vest in the owner.

WITHHOLDING PAYMENT TO CONTRACTOR.

In addition to the retainage, the owner may withhold or reduce payments, including but not limited to final payment, in its sole discretion if any of the following exist:

> The work is not proceeding a) in accordance with the construction documents, including the approved schedule, or b) as anticipated by the project consultant or the owner. In that event, the project consultant or the owner will assess the anticipated delay, and the owner will use the amounts specified for liquidated damages as the basis for amounts withheld. By making

said funds available to contractor, owner does not waive its right to assess liquidated damages at the completion of the project;

Liquidated damages as set forth in this contract;

Defective work unremedied;

Punch-list items unremedied;

Subject to the owner's written notice to contractor in accordance with the contract documents, back charge items for work performed by the owner or another contractor at the request of owner that is within the scope of the work under this construction contract;

Claims filed by subcontractors, laborers, suppliers, materialmen, or others;

Failure to comply with any and all insurance requirements;

Failure of the contractor to make payment properly to subcontractors or others;

Damage to the owner or to another contractor;

Reasonable evidence that the work will not be completed on or before the substantial completion or final completion date;

Failure of the contractor to carry out any of its obligations in accordance with the contract documents; and

Failure of the contractor to submit the information or documents required by this contract or reasonably required by the owner, including but not limited to schedules and daily logs.

CONTRACTOR'S RIGHT UPON NONPAYMENT.

If within thirty (30) days of the date payment to the contractor is due, the owner, without cause or basis hereunder, fails to pay the contractor any amounts then due and payable to the contractor, the contractor shall have the right to cease work until receipt of proper payment after first providing the owner with ten (10) days written notice of its intent to cease work.

DUTIES, OBLIGATIONS, AND RESPONSIBILITIES OF THE CONTRACTOR.

The contractor shall perform the work in accordance with the contract documents.

The contractor shall supervise the work and bear full responsibility for any and all acts or omissions of those engaged in the work on behalf of the contractor.

The contractor hereby warrants that all labor provided under this contract shall be competent to perform the tasks undertaken, that the product of such labor shall yield only first-class results, that all material and equipment provided shall be new and of high quality, and that the work will be complete, of high quality, without defects, and in compliance with the requirements of the contract documents. Any work not complying with the requirements of this subparagraph shall constitute a breach of the contractor's warranty.

The contractor shall obtain and pay for all required permits, fees, and licenses and shall comply with all legal requirements applicable to the work.

The contractor shall maintain a submittal log which shall include, at a minimum, the date of each submittal, the date of any resubmittal, the date of any approval or rejection, and the reason for any approval or rejection.

At all times, the contractor shall permit the owner and the project consultant to enter the project site and to review or inspect the work.

CLAIMS BY THE CONTRACTOR.

Although the contractor acknowledges the no damage for delay clause, in the event the contractor is entitled to assert a claim against owner for any reason, claims by the contractor against the owner are subject to the following terms and conditions:

All contractor claims against the owner shall be initiated by a written claim submitted to the owner and the project consultant. The owner and the project consultant shall receive the claim no later than fifteen calendar days after the event, or the first appearance of the circumstances causing the claim. The claim shall set forth in detail all known facts and circumstances supporting the claim and the actual damages or injuries suffered.

The contractor shall continue its performance of this contract regardless of any claims submitted by the contractor.

The contractor shall strictly comply with the notice requirements above and shall make the claim before executing any additional or changed work. Failure to provide the required notice shall constitute a complete waiver by the contractor of any claim for additional compensation or extension of time. This written notice requirement may not be waived by verbal representations or the acts of representatives of the owner or project consultant.

In connection with any claim by the contractor against the owner for compensation in excess of the contract price, any liability of the owner for the contractor's cost shall be strictly limited to direct cost of labor and materials incurred by the contractor at the jobsite and shall in no event include indirect cost, overhead, loss of profit, or consequential damages of the contractor. The owner shall not be liable to the contractor for claims of third parties including, but not limited to, subcontractors, suppliers, laborers, etc.

CHANGE ORDERS.

The contractor shall proceed with any extra work or changes which alter the contract by adding to, or deducting from, the contract sum or contract time in strict accordance with the following terms and conditions.

Change order means a written order to the contractor executed by the owner and the project consultant, after execution of this contract, directing a change in the work and may include a change in the contract sum or the time for the contractor's performance, or both.

Any change in the contract sum or time resulting from a change order shall be determined as follows:

> By mutual agreement between the owner and the contractor as evidenced by a) the change in the contract price or time being set forth in change order and b) the execution of the change order; or
>
> If no mutual agreement occurs between the owner and the contractor, the change in the contract sum, if any, shall be derived based upon the cost-plus price by determining the total actual costs incurred or savings achieved, resulting from revisions in the work. The total actual costs or savings shall include a component for direct jobsite overhead and profit but under no circumstances shall it include non-jobsite overhead expenses or costs or any other indirect costs or components. Any such costs or savings shall be documented in the format, and with such content and detail, as the owner or the project consultant requires. If agreement is not reached as to the change in time, contractor shall be given a reasonable time based upon the scope of work required by the change.

The execution of a change order by the contractor shall constitute conclusive evidence of the contractor's agreement to the ordered changes in the work and the change in the contract, price, and the time for performance by the contractor. By executing the change order, the contractor waives and forever releases any claim against the owner for additional time or compensation for issues or matters relating to or arising out of or resulting from the work included within or affected by the executed change order.

The owner, without invalidating the contract, may require a change for any reason whatsoever.

All such work shall be executed under the terms of the original contract.

All change orders and adjustments shall be in writing and executed by the contractor and owner; otherwise, no claim for additional compensation or time will be allowed.

The value of any change ordered under the contract for extra work and/or any reductions in required work shall be determined under one or more of the following procedures before a written change order is issued.

By **unit prices** named in the contract or subsequently agreed upon by the owner and the contractor, which prices shall include contractor's overhead and profit.

By an agreed **lump sum price** based upon actual reasonable costs and direct jobsite overhead by the owner and the contractor. This price shall include the contractor's overhead and profit but under no circumstances shall it include non-jobsite overhead, expenses, or costs or any other indirect costs.

The project consultant may require a breakdown of the estimated costs comprising the lump sum price for review.

OVERHEAD AND PROFIT.

Percentage for overhead and profit shall be determined in accordance with the method listed for **cost plus price**, based on total actual costs, plus an added percentage, all determined as follows.

JOBSITE OVERHEAD, including supervision and the furnishing, use and maintenance of small tools, and ordinary equipment incidental to and required for the work of **subcontractors** (whether performed by them or others) shall be considered to be just and fully compensated for, by adding an amount equal to 5 percent of the sum of material costs, labor costs, and rentals. There shall be no compensation for any non-jobsite overhead, expenses, or costs.

PROFIT may then be added by the subcontractor to the above material costs and labor costs, including the JOBSITE OVERHEAD allowance, at the rate of 10 percent of the sum of those costs.

JOBSITE OVERHEAD, including general supervision and the furnishing, use, and maintenance of small equipment incidental to and required for the work of the contractor (including that of his subcontractors) shall be considered to be just and fully compensated for by adding an amount equal to 10 percent of the sum of material costs, labor, and rentals. There shall be no compensation for any non-jobsite overhead expenses or costs.

PROFIT may then be added by the contractor to the above material costs and labor costs, including the jobsite overhead allowance, at the rate of 5 percent of the sum of those costs.

BOND ALLOWANCE for maintaining the performance bond at 100 percent of the contract amount, a sum of 1 percent of the total cost of the change, (including material, labor, overhead and profit, and equipment rentals) shall be allowed on all change orders.

The total actual costs of materials, labor, and equipment rentals may include the following only:

> Material costs actually recorded by the contractor and/or subcontractors as they are delivered to the site and as evidenced from originally receipted invoices, listing appropriate quantities and unit prices. The contractor shall maintain records in proper form and make them available to the project consultant at all times.
>
> Labor costs represented by the actual wages paid to all laborers, apprentices, journeymen, and foremen involved in and necessary to completing the particular construction operations, for each day and every hour such laborers and foremen are actually employed and on the extra work required, including the net cost of insurance, social security, and workers' compensation. The furnishing, use, and maintenance of small tools and ordinary equipment normal to the work of individual workmen in the trades will be considered part of the labor costs. The contractor shall maintain records in proper form and make them available to the project consultant at all times.

> <u>Rentals</u> for special equipment or machinery such as power driven rollers, tractors, trucks, shovels, drills, mixers, pumps, hoists, etc., required for the economical performance of the work, at reasonable rental prices agreed upon before work commences, shall be allowed the contractor and/or its subcontractors by the project consultant for each and every hour such special equipment is in use on the particular work.

The contractor is obligated to proceed with the work that is the subject of a change order, even though the contractor and owner have not agreed to an adjustment to the contract price or time, and even if the parties are disputing the change order. A change order or proposed change order shall not be the basis of the contractor not performing pursuant to the contract documents.

The project consultant will have authority to order minor changes in the work not involving an adjustment to the contract sum or contract time and not inconsistent with the intent of the contract documents. Such changes shall be affected by written order and such changes shall be binding on the owner and the contractor.

The owner has authorized the following approval thresholds for change orders in the name of the School Board of Nita County under Board Policy 7006, the rules of which are incorporated below:

- A) The superintendent or the associate superintendent of facilities and construction management is authorized to approve change orders up to the cumulative total of 5 percent of the original construction contract amount.
- B) When the cumulative total of all change orders on a project has exceeded the ceiling, all subsequent change orders will require prior board approval, except in emergency cases as declared by the superintendent, or where the change order in question would be in the form of a credit, thereby reducing the adjusted contract amount.
- C) Approval of change orders under this policy shall be for the purposes of expediting the work in progress and shall be confirmed by board action at the next regular meeting of the board.

DISCOVERING AND CORRECTING DEFECTIVE OR INCOMPLETE WORK.

In the event that the contractor covers, conceals, or obscures its work in violation of this contract or in violation of a directive from the owner or the project consultant, such work shall be uncovered and displayed for the owner's or project consultant's inspection upon request, and shall be reworked at no cost in time or money to the owner.

If the uncovered work conforms substantially with this contract, the costs incurred by the contractor to uncover and subsequently replace such work shall be borne by the owner; otherwise, such costs shall be borne by the contractor.

The contractor shall, at no additional cost to the owner or extension of time, correct work rejected by the owner or by the project consultant as defective or failing to conform to this contract. Additionally, the contractor shall reimburse the owner for all testing, inspections, and other expenses incurred as a result thereof.

In addition to its warranty obligations set forth elsewhere herein, the contractor shall be specifically obligated to correct any and all defective or nonconforming work for a period of twelve months following final completion upon written direction from the owner.

The owner may, but shall in no event be required to, choose to accept defective or nonconforming work. In such event, the owner has the option of reducing the contract price by the greater of 1) the reasonable costs of removing and correcting the defective or nonconforming work, or 2) the difference between the fair market value of the project as constructed and the fair market value of the project had its construction not included defective or nonconforming work.

If the remaining portion of the unpaid contract price, if any, is insufficient to compensate the owner for accepting defective or nonconforming work, the contractor shall, upon written demand from the owner, pay the owner the remaining compensation for accepting defective or nonconforming work.

GOVERNING LAW.

The construction contract shall be governed by the laws of the State of Nita.

Exhibit 2

List of Prior Invoices Paid to Brett General Contracting, LLC

Brett General Contracting, LLC
21 Chelsea Court
Nita City, Nita 57819
(819) 555-7688

STATEMENT OF INVOICES 9.19.YR-4

Project Name: Nita Public High School, 1500 Nita Road, Nita City, Nita 57818

Project No. 48022

Invoice Date	Change Order #	Invoice Amount for Delayed Costs	Delay Cost Description	Invoice Status	Date Paid by SBNC
2.4.YR-4	1	14,892.01	Demo and Permits	Paid in Full	2.28.19
3.18.YR-4	2	20,241.05	Materials (Concrete and Glass)	Paid in Full	4.12.19
5.20.YR-4	3	38,022.72	Equipment Rental	Paid in Full	6.14.19
6.17.YR-4	4	17,940.18	Storage Fees—Hurricane	Paid in Full	7.12.19
8.12.YR-4	5	54,252.06	Payroll—Hurricane	Paid in Full	9.19.19
Total		$145,348.02		Paid in Full	9.19.19

Exhibit 3

FIRST CHANGE ORDER, APRIL 22, YR-3

School Board of Nita County

Office of Facilities & Construction

888 Main Avenue, Rm 213
Nita City, Nita 57812
(819) 555-3857

Document 01250g (00 63 63)-Construction Change Order #01

Facility Name:	Alan B. Whitfield Elementary School	Date:	4/22/YR-3
Project Name:	Project 50225 FY-3–FY-2—Project 8 Classroom Additions and Cafeteria Remodel	Project #	50225
Location No:			
Contractor:	Brett General Contracting, LLC	Reference Letter Dated:	NA

Description of Change: Supplemental modifications to plans for internal wiring and framing supplies

Attachments NA

Reason for Change: Adjustments made due to updating plans to modify electrical wiring and framing required

Summary:

Total Credits and/or Added Costs:	Add:	$65,937.00
	Deduct:	$0

The Contract Time will remain unchanged.

THIS CHANGE ORDER ITEM IS INCLUSIVE OF ALL COSTS ASSOCIATED WITH THIS WORK. NO ADDITIONAL COMPENSATION FOR EXTENDED TIME SHALL BE DUE AS A RESULT OF THIS CHANGE IN THE SCOPE OF WORK.

Recommended		Accepted	
Sonia Forester	*04/22/YR-3*	*Richard Brett*	*4/22/YR-3*
Project Consultant's Signature	Date	Contractor's Signature	Date
Sonia Forester		Richard Brett	
Project Consultant's Typed Name		Contractor's Typed Name	
We Build Nita, Inc.		Brett General Contracting, LLC	
Project Consultant's Firm Name		Contractor's Firm Name	

Consultant Concurs with Categorization:

☐ Yes ☐ No

FOR OFFICE USE ONLY

Direct Owner Purchase (DOP)

☐ Owner's Request ☐ Unforeseen ☐ Consultant Error ☒ Consultant Omission ☐ Direct Owner Purchase ☐ Tax Savings

The School Board of Nita County
P.001729

Document 01250g (00 63 63)
Construction Change Order
Page 1 of 1

Composite Exhibit 4

June 24, YR-3, Email from Brett Submitting Change Order #2 to PM Smith

Richard Brett

FROM:	Brett, Richard <RichardB@GC.nita>
DATE:	June 24, YR-3 4:12 PM
TO:	Smith, Thomas <TSmith@SBNC.nita>
RE:	Change Order #2
ATTACH:	Chg2.docx

Dear Tom, Hope you are well. As you are aware, due to the delays caused by SBNC, I have incurred additional expenses that I have had to pay out of pocket. These expenses include storage, staffing, and equipment rentals and they are all included on the attached change order, as required by the contract.

I would very much appreciate if you would approve the change order ASAP so that I can be reimbursed.

Thanks,

Richard

Office of Facilities & Construction
888 Main Avenue, Rm 213
Nita City, Nita 57812
(819) 555-3857

School Board of Nita County

Document 01250g (00 63 63)-Construction Change Order #02

Facility Name: Alan B. Whitfield Elementary School — Date: 6/24/YR-3

Project Name: Project 50225 FY-3–FY-2—Project 8 Classroom Additions and Cafeteria Remodel — Project # 50225

Location No:

Contractor: Brett General Contracting, LLC — Reference Letter Dated: NA

Description of Change: Additional Costs Outlined on Attachment Paid Out of Pocket Due to Delays on Project

Attachments NA

Reason for Change: See attachment

Summary:

Total Credits and/or Added Costs: Add: $195,214.88

Deduct: $0

The Contract Time has been updated

THIS CHANGE ORDER ITEM IS INCLUSIVE OF ALL COSTS ASSOCIATED WITH THIS WORK. NO ADDITIONAL COMPENSATION FOR EXTENDED TIME SHALL BE DUE AS A RESULT OF THIS CHANGE IN THE SCOPE OF WORK.

Recommended	Accepted
	Richard Brett 6/24/YR-3
Project Consultant's Signature — Date	Contractor's Signature — Date
Sonia Forester	Richard Brett
Project Consultant's Typed Name	Contractor's Typed Name
We Build Nita, Inc.	Brett General Contracting, LLC
Project Consultant's Firm Name	Contractor's Firm Name

Consultant Concurs with Categorization:

☐ Yes ☐ No

FOR OFFICE USE ONLY

Direct Owner Purchase (DOP)

☐ Owner's Request ☐ Unforeseen ☒ Consultant Error ☒ Consultant Omission ☐ Direct Owner Purchase ☐ Tax Savings

The School Board of Nita County
P.001729

Document 01250g (00 63 63)
Construction Change Order
Page 1 of 1

Brett General Contracting, LLC
21 Chelsea Court
Nita City, Nita 57819
(819) 555-7688

OUT OF POCKET COSTS

Project Name: Nita Public High School, 1500 Nita Road, Nita City, Nita 57818

Project No. 48022

Invoice Date	Change Order #	Invoice Amount for Delayed Costs	Delay Cost Description	Invoice Status	Date Paid by SBNC
4.29.YR-3	2	68,022.72	Equipment Rental – Tom Smith	Pending	
5.13.YR-3	2	52,940.10	Storage Fees – Smith/Pandemic	Pending	
5.27.YR-3	2	74,252.06	Payroll – Smith/Pandemic	Pending	
Total		$195,214.88		Pending	

Exhibit 5

Audio File
July 6, YR-3, Voicemail from PM Smith to Brett

Transcript

Hey Rich—Uh, sorry it's taken me a bit to get back to you. Uh, been ill, in the hospital, so I've been on PTO. I'm gonna take disability and there'll be a new project manager starting in a few weeks. Uh, but I know this is my delay, so I will go ahead and approve the change order and make sure you get paid before I leave. Thanks for your patience, buddy. Talk to you soon.

Composite Exhibit 6

September 3, YR-3, Email from Brett Submitting Change Order #2 to PM Marks

Richard Brett

FROM:	Brett, Richard <RichardB@GC.nita>
DATE:	September 3, YR-3 9:17 AM
TO:	Marks, Carol <CarolM@SBNC.nita>
RE:	Change Order #2 Past Due
ATTACH:	Chg2.docx

Dear Carol,

How are you?

Please see the attached 2nd change order, which I emailed to Tom back in June. Because of the delays from Tom being out sick and from the pandemic, I had to pay out of pocket some expenses including storage, staffing, and equipment rentals. Tom left me a voicemail before he left which said that he would make sure that I got paid, and acknowledging that the delay was not my fault. I still have not received any payment, and I would appreciate it if you would approve the change order ASAP so that I can be reimbursed.

Many thanks,

Richard

Office of Facilities & Construction

888 Main Avenue, Rm 213
Nita City, Nita 57812
(819) 555-3857

School Board
of Nita County

Document 01250g (00 63 63)-Construction Change Order #02

Facility Name:	Alan B. Whitfield Elementary School	Date:	6/24/YR-3
Project Name:	Project 50225 FY-3–FY-2—Project 8 Classroom Additions and Cafeteria Remodel	Project #	50225
Location No:			
Contractor:	Brett General Contracting, LLC	Reference Letter Dated:	NA

Description of Change: Additional Costs Outlined on Attachment Paid Out of Pocket Due to Delays on Project

Attachments NA

Reason for Change: See attachment

Summary:

Total Credits and/or Added Costs: Add: $195,214.88

Deduct: $0

The Contract Time has been updated

THIS CHANGE ORDER ITEM IS INCLUSIVE OF ALL COSTS ASSOCIATED WITH THIS WORK. NO ADDITIONAL COMPENSATION FOR EXTENDED TIME SHALL BE DUE AS A RESULT OF THIS CHANGE IN THE SCOPE OF WORK.

Recommended		Accepted	
		Richard Brett	*6/24/YR-3*
Project Consultant's Signature	Date	Contractor's Signature	Date
Sonia Forester		Richard Brett	
Project Consultant's Typed Name		Contractor's Typed Name	
We Build Nita, Inc.		Brett General Contracting, LLC	
Project Consultant's Firm Name		Contractor's Firm Name	

Consultant Concurs with Categorization:

☐ Yes ☐ No

FOR OFFICE USE ONLY

Direct Owner Purchase (DOP)

☐ Owner's Request ☐ Unforeseen ☒ Consultant Error ☒ Consultant Omission ☐Direct Owner Purchase ☐ Tax Savings

The School Board of Nita County
P.001729

Document 01250g (00 63 63)
Construction Change Order
Page 1 of 1

Brett General Contracting, LLC
21 Chelsea Court
Nita City, Nita 57819
(819) 555-7688

OUT OF POCKET COSTS

Project Name: Nita Public High School, 1500 Nita Road, Nita City, Nita 57818

Project No. 48022

Invoice Date	Change Order #	Invoice Amount for Delayed Costs	Delay Cost Description	Invoice Status	Date Paid by SBNC
4.29.YR-3	2	68,022.72	Equipment Rental – Tom Smith	Pending	
5.13.YR-3	2	52,940.10	Storage Fees – Smith/Pandemic	Pending	
5.27.YR-3	2	74,252.06	Payroll – Smith/Pandemic	Pending	
Total		$195,214.88		Pending	

Exhibit 7

January 19, YR-2, Post-it Note from Marks to Brett

Richard, fyi,
SBNC said they'll
pay the CO.
stay tuned.

Exhibit 8

February 22, YR-2, Letter from School Board to Brett

School Board
of Nita County

888 Main Avenue, Rm 200
Nita City, Nita 57812
(819) 555-3855

February 22, YR-2

Brett General Contracting, LLC
c/o Richard Brett

Dear Mr. Brett:

This letter is to inform you that it has come to my attention that you are requesting a change order be approved. Please note that we have not seen a change order. Therefore, the School Board of Nita County has denied payment and request for extra time of the final change order, dated 6.24.YR-3, specifically due to the following:

1) The project manager did not have authority to approve any payment for delays without the SBNC's approval;

2) The change order was never on the SBNC's board meeting agenda; and

3) There is a no-damages-for-delay clause in the contract.

Given the aforementioned, the CO request is denied. We expect the project to be completed in due course, in line with the deadlines stated in the contract.

Sincerely,
Holly Williams
SBNC Board Member

Exhibit [illegible]

[illegible]

Ref: [illegible]

[illegible]

[illegible]

[illegible]

Composite Exhibit 9

Emails from PM Marks to Brett

Richard Brett

FROM:	Marks, Carol <CarolM@SBNC.nita>
DATE:	June 23, YR-2 4:58 PM
TO:	Brett, Richard <RichardB@GC.nita>
RE:	FW: Status Update—Completion

Hi Richard, please advise as to when we can expect FINAL completion of project. While I am glad that you have finished the classrooms, we do still need the cafeteria done before the beginning of the next school year, which, again, is Monday, August 24th, YR-2. That is two months from now, so we really need to get this finished.

Carol

Richard Brett

FROM:	Marks, Carol <CarolM@SBNC.nita>
DATE:	April 22, YR-2 12:42 PM
TO:	Brett, Richard <RichardB@GC.nita>
RE:	Status Update—Completion

Hi Richard, please advise as to ETA re: completion of Project. As you know, per the contract, final completion of the Project must be before the beginning of the next school year, which is Monday, August 24th, YR-2. Thank you in advance for your reply.

Carol

Composite Exhibit 10

LETTERS FROM BRETT TO SCHOOL BOARD RE: FINAL COMPLETION

Brett General Contracting, LLC
21 Chelsea Court
Nita City, Nita 57819
(819) 555-7688

June 20, YR-2

The School Board of Nita County
c/o Marsha Stewart, Esq.
Stewart Law, PA

Dear Ms. Stewart,

I am pleased to inform you that all of the eight classrooms for 1532 Nita Road, Nita City, Nita 57818 have been completed.

Please advise if you have any questions.

Thank you,

Richard Brett

Brett General Contracting, LLC

Brett General Contracting, LLC
21 Chelsea Court
Nita City, Nita 57819
(819) 555-7688

August 17, YR-2

The School Board of Nita County
c/o Marsha Stewart, Esq.
Stewart Law, PA

Dear Ms. Stewart,

I am pleased to inform you that all project work, including the cafeteria for 1532 Nita Road, Nita City, Nita 57818, has now been completed. Attached please find the final invoice, which includes the delayed payments for the 2nd change order.

As you have been made aware, both Tom Smith and Carol Marks previously approved the change order, but it has yet to be paid. Given that I have completed the project in good faith, I am requesting quick payment of this change order.

If there is anything else that you need from me in order to effectuate this payment, please let me know.

Thank you,

Richard Brett

Brett General Contracting, LLC

School Board of Nita County

Office of Facilities & Construction

888 Main Avenue, Rm 213
Nita City, Nita 57812
(819) 555-3857

Document 01250g (00 63 63)-Construction Change Order #02

Facility Name: Alan B. Whitfield Elementary School — Date: 6/24/YR-3

Project Name: Project 50225 FY-3–FY-2—Project 8 Classroom Additions and Cafeteria Remodel — Project # 50225

Location No:

Contractor: Brett General Contracting, LLC — Reference Letter Dated: NA

Description of Change: Additional Costs Outlined on Attachment Paid Out of Pocket Due to Delays on Project

Attachments NA

Reason for Change: See attachment

Summary:

Total Credits and/or Added Costs: Add: $195,214.88 Deduct: $0

The Contract Time has been updated

THIS CHANGE ORDER ITEM IS INCLUSIVE OF ALL COSTS ASSOCIATED WITH THIS WORK. NO ADDITIONAL COMPENSATION FOR EXTENDED TIME SHALL BE DUE AS A RESULT OF THIS CHANGE IN THE SCOPE OF WORK.

Recommended		Accepted	
		Richard Brett	6/24/YR-3
Project Consultant's Signature	Date	Contractor's Signature	Date
Sonia Forester		Richard Brett	
Project Consultant's Typed Name		Contractor's Typed Name	
We Build Nita, Inc.		Brett General Contracting, LLC	
Project Consultant's Firm Name		Contractor's Firm Name	

Consultant Concurs with Categorization:

☐ Yes ☐ No

FOR OFFICE USE ONLY

☐ Owner's Request ☐ Unforeseen ☒ Consultant Error ☒ Consultant Omission

Direct Owner Purchase (DOP)

☐ Direct Owner Purchase ☐ Tax Savings

The School Board of Nita County
P.001729

Document 01250g (00 63 63)
Construction Change Order
Page 1 of 1

Brett General Contracting, LLC
21 Chelsea Court
Nita City, Nita 57819
(819) 555-7688

OUT OF POCKET COSTS

Project Name: Nita Public High School, 1500 Nita Road, Nita City, Nita 57818

Project No. 48022

Invoice Date	Change Order #	Invoice Amount for Delayed Costs	Delay Cost Description	Invoice Status	Date Paid by SBNC
4.29.YR-3	2	68,022.72	Equipment Rental – Tom Smith	Pending	
5.13.YR-3	2	52,940.10	Storage Fees – Smith/Pandemic	Pending	
5.27.YR-3	2	74,252.06	Payroll – Smith/Pandemic	Pending	
Total		$195,214.88		Pending	

Composite Exhibit 11

School Board Meeting Minutes Dated May 3, YR-3, Approving First Change Order

SCHOOL BOARD OF NITA COUNTY
OFFICE OF THE SUPERINTENDENT
May 3, YR-3
Thursday, 9:05 a.m.
MINUTES OF SPECIAL SESSION MEETING

The School Board of Nita County, Nita, met in special session at 9:10 a.m. in the board room of the School Board of Nita County Administrative Center, 888 Main Avenue, Nita City, Nita.

Present were school board members Jeff Shaw, chair; Barbara Horton, vice chair; Thomas Johnson; Brenda Hart, Esq.; Daniel Fabliani; Dr. Charles T. Hoffman; and Holly Williams.

Call to Order: The chair called the meeting to order. Secretary Ms. Wendy Freedman led the Pledge of Allegiance to the Flag of the United States of America.

<u>00-01. Project 50225 FY-3-YR-2-Project8 Classroom Additions and Cafeteria Remodel</u>

Change Order #1-Alan B. Whitfield Elementary School
(Approved)

Motion was made by Mrs. Horton, seconded by Mr. Fabiani, and carried, to approve change order #1 in the amount of $65,937.00 and no change to the contract duration—Brett General Contracting, LLC, Alan B. Whitfield Elementary School Renovations, Project No. 50225, 1532 Nita Road, Nita City, Nita 57818 (6-0 vote).

No discussion was held and a vote was taken on this item.

No further items for discussion at this time. This meeting was adjourned at 10:15 a.m.

Check Dated May 2, YR-3 Paying First Change Order

School Board of Nita County 2815

Date May 2, YR-3

Pay to the Order of Brett General Contracting, LLC $ 65,937.00

Sixty-five thousand nine hundred thirty seven Dollars

Memo Pr50225-CO#1 Jeff Shaw

⑆85871713 ⑆186358875718⑆ 11638

Potential Exhibits

April 8, YR-1 Declaration of Sonia Forester, We Build Nita, Inc.

IN THE STATE OF NITA
NITA COUNTY CIRCUIT COURT

BRETT GENERAL CONTRACTING, LLC, a Nita corporation, Plaintiff, v. THE SCHOOL BOARD OF NITA COUNTY, Defendant.	CASE NO. 2-31869(12)(B)

DECLARATION OF SONIA FORESTER, WE BUILD NITA, INC.

1. I am over the age of 18 and not a party to the above-styled action.
2. I am a certified professional architect in the State of Nita, and I am the owner of We Build Nita, Inc.
3. This declaration is based on my personal knowledge of plans and drawings I prepared for the School Board of Nita County ("SBNC").
4. On September 1, YR-5, I prepared drawings of plans to be relied upon for multiple renovation projects for the SBNC.
5. Those drawing(s) were the same design to be used for renovations in both School Board of Nita County projects No. 48022 and No. 50225.
6. On a prior SBNC construction project No. 48022, these same drawings were relied upon by the general contractor, Brett General Contracting, LLC, there were no design defects in these drawings and on the prior project No. 48022, however there were delays due to the lack of responsiveness from the SBNC's project managers.
7. I specifically recall that on this project, Project No. 50225, the general contractor reached out on several occasions with recommended modifications to the design drawings and the SBNC project managers were, again, lax in responding.

FURTHER AFFIANT SAYETH NAUGHT.

Sonia Forester

Sonia Forester
April 8, YR-1

January 27, YR-2 Text Messages Between Brett and Smith

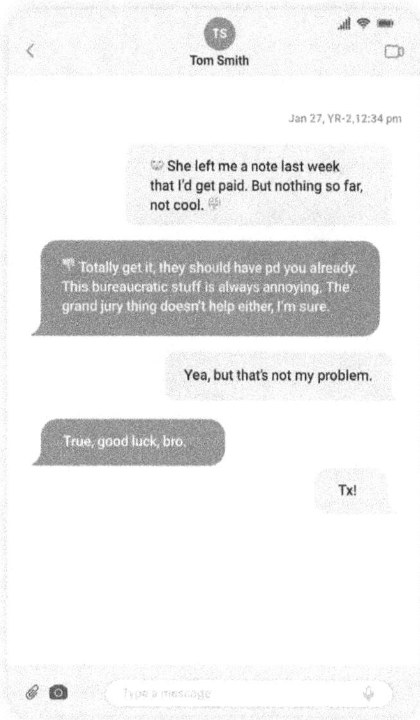

JANUARY 15, YR-2 SNAPTALK POST BY RICHARD BRETT REGARDING DELAYS AND NONPAYMENT

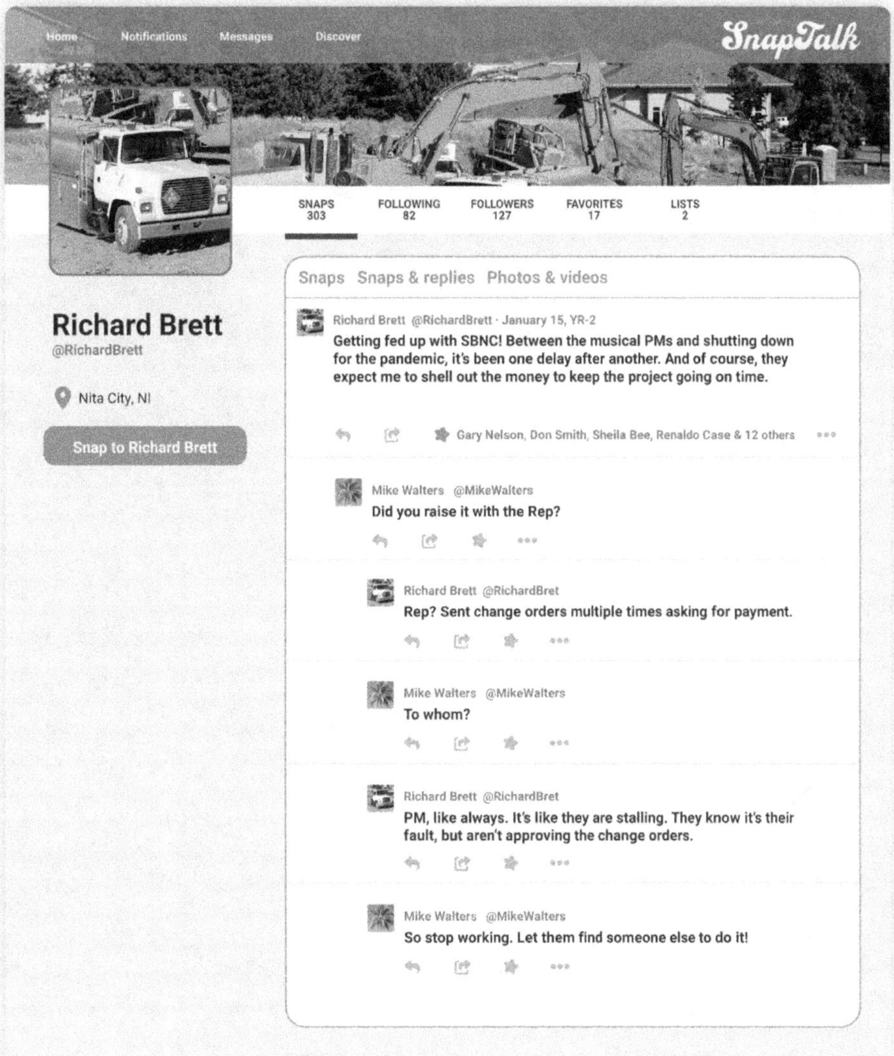

Home Notifications Messages Discover

SnapTalk

SNAPS 303 FOLLOWING 82 FOLLOWERS 127 FAVORITES 17 LISTS 2

Snaps Snaps & replies Photos & videos

Richard Brett
@RichardBrett

Nita City, NI

Snap to Richard Brett

Richard Brett @RichardBrett · January 15, YR-2
Getting fed up with SBNC! Between the musical PMs and shutting down for the pandemic, it's been one delay after another. And of course, they expect me to shell out the money to keep the project going on time.

Gary Nelson, Don Smith, Sheila Bee, Renaldo Case & 12 others

Mike Walters @MikeWalters
Did you raise it with the Rep?

Richard Brett @RichardBret
Rep? Sent change orders multiple times asking for payment.

Mike Walters @MikeWalters
To whom?

Richard Brett @RichardBret
PM, like always. It's like they are stalling. They know it's their fault, but aren't approving the change orders.

Mike Walters @MikeWalters
So stop working. Let them find someone else to do it!

November 2, YR-3 SnapTalk Post by Carol Marks Regarding Project Delays

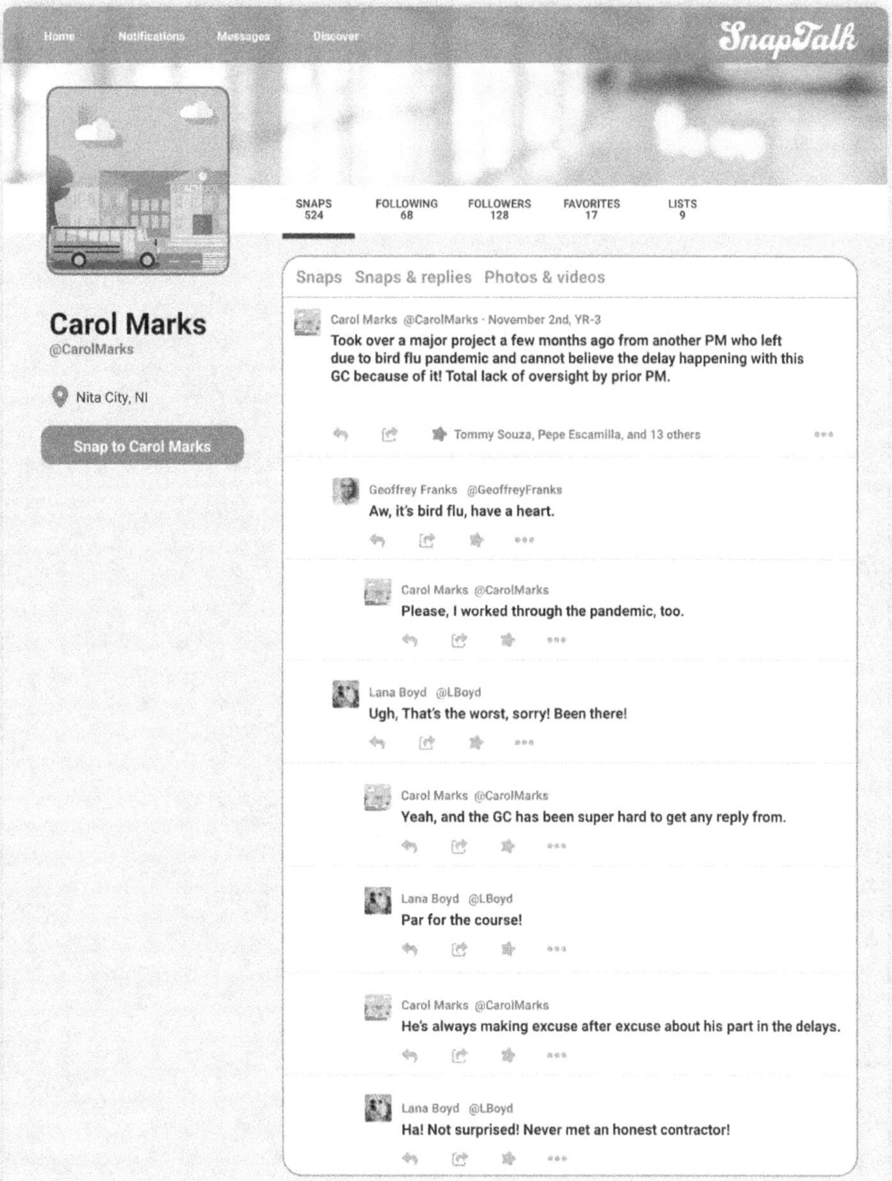
Home Notifications Messages Discover
SnapTalk
SNAPS 524 FOLLOWING 68 FOLLOWERS 128 FAVORITES 17 LISTS 9
Snaps Snaps & replies Photos & videos

Carol Marks
@CarolMarks
Nita City, NI
Snap to Carol Marks

Carol Marks @CarolMarks · November 2nd, YR-3
Took over a major project a few months ago from another PM who left due to bird flu pandemic and cannot believe the delay happening with this GC because of it! Total lack of oversight by prior PM.
Tommy Souza, Pepe Escamilla, and 13 others

Geoffrey Franks @GeoffreyFranks
Aw, it's bird flu, have a heart.

Carol Marks @CarolMarks
Please, I worked through the pandemic, too.

Lana Boyd @LBoyd
Ugh, That's the worst, sorry! Been there!

Carol Marks @CarolMarks
Yeah, and the GC has been super hard to get any reply from.

Lana Boyd @LBoyd
Par for the course!

Carol Marks @CarolMarks
He's always making excuse after excuse about his part in the delays.

Lana Boyd @LBoyd
Ha! Not surprised! Never met an honest contractor!

January 15, YR-3 We Build Nita Classroom Plans

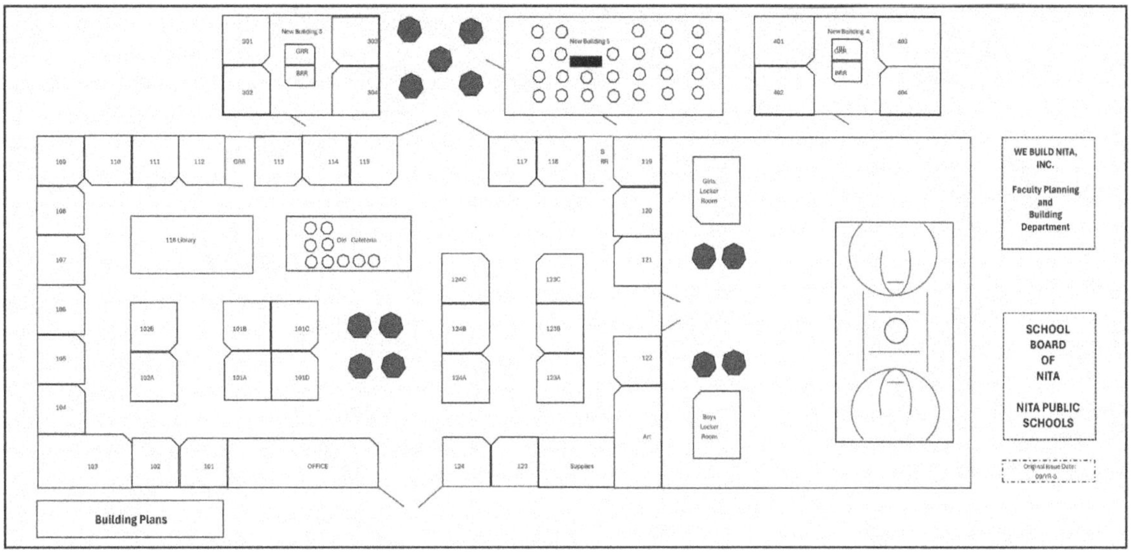

August 26, YR-5 *Nita County Gazette* Newspaper Article

Subscribe

NITA COUNTY GAZETTE

Top story

Grand Jury: The School Board of Nita County Spent 3 MIL of Taxpayer Money Without Votes

August 24, YR-5

A Grand Jury came back with a verdict against the School Board of Nita County, declaring that the school board wasted millions of taxpayer money paying construction contracts that contractors were not entitled to receive. The judge ruled that the school board must hire in-house counsel to review any future contracts and perform audits.

Attorney Marsha Stewart, whose firm was hired to oversee a routine audit, first noticed that the school board had been paying for delays even though they have a no-damages-for-delay clause in their contracts. She brought this to the attention of the school board, which put an end to the practice going forward. But taxpayers discovered the payments and brought this action against the school board.

Thanks to her audit work, the school board has now hired Ms. Stewart to serve as in-house counsel. A final hearing on the fine to be imposed upon the School Board of Nita County will be scheduled for next month.

Timeline for Participants

TIMELINE OF EVENTS

Date	Event Description
08.26.YR-5	Newspaper article in *Nita County Gazette* about Grand Jury findings that School Board of Nita County wasted millions of taxpayer money paying construction contracts that the contractors were not entitled to receive.
09.19.YR-4	Depo Exhibit 2: Brett General Contracting, LLC statement listing invoices with prior jobs outlined and stamped PAID by SBNC.
03.10.YR-3	Depo Exhibit 1: contract executed between Brett General Contracting, LLC and the School Board of Nita County
03.10.YR-3	1st SBNC project manager, Thomas Smith, joins the project
03.12.YR-3	Brett receives drawings previously prepared by architect Sonia Forester, We Build Nita, Inc.
04.01.YR-3	Brett commences work on project
04.22.YR-3	Depo Exhibit 3: Brett submits first change order to Smith
05.02.YR-3	Depo Exhibit 11: School board issues check paying first change order
05.03.YR-3	Depo Exhibit 11: School board approves first change order
06.24.YR-3	Depo Composite Exhibit 4: 06.24.YR-3 email submitting second change order to Smith
07.06.YR-3	Depo Exhibit 5: Smith leaves Brett a voice mail admitting he will get him some money
08.03.YR-3	Second SBNC project manager, Carol Marks, joins the project
09.03.YR-3	Depo Composite Exhibit 6: 09.3.YR-3 email from Brett to Marks resubmitting second change order
11.02.YR-3	Social media post by Marks relating to taking over a project in serious delay by contractor
01.15.YR-2	Social media post by Brett about delays
01.19.YR-2	Depo Exhibit 7: Marks leaves handwritten note for Brett
02.22.YR-2	Depo Exhibit 8: Letter from SBNC board member Holly Williams advising Brett that SBNC has denied payment.
01.15.YR-2	Text exchange between Brett and Smith regarding payment delays
04.22.YR-2	Depo Exhibit 9: Marks emails Brett requesting ETA on project completion

06.20.YR-2	Depo Exhibit 10: Brett sends letter to SBNC's attorney, Marsha Stewart, Esq. notifying school board of partial completion of the project
06.20.YR-2	Deadline for completion of substantial work per the agreement
06.23.YR-2	Depo Exhibit 9: Marks emails Brett about project completion
07.21.YR-2	Deadline for completion of final work per the agreement
08.17.YR-2	Depo Exhibit 10: Brett sends letter to Marsha Stewart, Esq. notifying school board of final completion of the project and resubmitting 2nd change order
08.20.YR-2	Final inspection; 2nd project manager approves completion
08.24.YR-2	New school year commences
10.01.YR-2	Complaint filed by Brett General Contracting, LLC against the School Board of Nita County
12.15.YR-2	Answer, Affirmative Defenses and Counterclaim filed by the School Board of Nita County
12.29.YR-2	Answer to Counterclaim filed by Brett General Contracting, LLC
04.02.YR-1	Depo of GC Richard Brett
04.02.YR-1	Depo of Def. Exp. Eric Mayper
04.03.YR-1	Depo of PM#1 Thomas Smith
04.03.YR-1	Depo of PM#2 Carol Marks
04.03.YR-1	Depo of SBNC board member Holly Williams
04.08.YR-1	Sonia Forester makes her affidavit

About the Authors

Marni Becker-Avin is an attorney and trial consultant. She has worked at Becker & Poliakoff, PA, which is among the largest firms in NITA, for 25 years. She is also the firm's Professional Development Director and Marketing Administrator. In this role, she created Becker & Poliakoff University (BPU), an annual educational immersion course, in which the attorneys at the firm utilize NITA case studies to hone their skills. Marni credits her father, Alan S. Becker, for making education a priority, and instilling in her a drive to help others succeed. Before he passed in 2020, Mr. Becker would regularly attend BPU and was fond of saying that he learned at least one new thing during every program.

Beth Thomas has over 40 years of experience as a litigation paralegal, specializing in evidence collection, organization, analysis, and procedures for use and admissions at trial. She has been with Becker & Poliakoff for 23 years. She has extensive trial experience in both Federal and State Courts. As Becker & Poliakoff's Director of Litigation Technology & Support, Ms. Thomas led the introduction and implementation of the firm's Uniform Case Management System for all litigation matters and electronic case management, created and manages the Firm's internal Litigation Support Department for the collection, processing and organization of all case evidence, has spearheaded the continued training of the Firm's litigation paralegal team, and is a Certified Trainer for Trial Director, a trial presentation software. Ms. Thomas plays an integral role in keeping the firm's litigation group on the cutting edge of eDiscovery and preservation of evidence.

www.ingramcontent.com/pod-product-compliance
Lightning Source LLC
LaVergne TN
LVHW082334200926
848481LV00012B/3339